SOUTH

SOUTH
The Endurance Expedition

SIR ERNEST SHACKLETON

INTRODUCTION BY GRETCHEN LEGLER

BARNES & NOBLE
NEW YORK

THE BARNES & NOBLE
LIBRARY OF ESSENTIAL READING

Introduction and Suggested Reading
© 2008 by Barnes & Noble, Inc.

Originally published in 1919

This 2008 edition published by Barnes & Noble, Inc.

Barnes & Noble, Inc.
122 Fifth Avenue
New York, NY 10011

ISBN-13: 978-0-7607-8662-8
ISBN-10: 0-7607-8662-3

Printed and bound in the United States of America

1 3 5 7 9 10 8 6 4 2

Contents

INTRODUCTION

S<small>IR</small> E<small>RNEST</small> H<small>ENRY</small> S<small>HACKLETON</small>'<small>S</small> <small>EXPEDITIONS IN THE</small> A<small>NTARCTIC</small> for almost a hundred years have captured the hearts and imaginations of armchair explorers, passionate adventurers, scientists, historians of the Antarctic, and most recently, even stockbrokers and CEOs, who laud Shackleton's skills as a visionary and an exemplary leader. Many excellent books, movies, television specials, and reprints of expedition members' diaries and letters have recounted for popular audiences the details of Shackleton's extraordinary 1914–1917 Imperial Trans-Antarctic Expedition—the expedition that brought to a close the Heroic Age of Antarctic exploration. *South*, however, is the story in Ernest Shackleton's *own* words.

The story of the *Endurance* is one that still defies imagination. In this extraordinary nonfiction tale, we hear the steady, understated, optimistic tone of "The Boss," as he narrates one of the most spectacular adventure sagas of all time. It's a survival tale of fortitude, of navigational magic, of mountaineering expertise, and of spiritual wonder. Mountain climbers still marvel at how Shackleton, Frank Worsley, and Thomas Crean made it from King Haakon Bay over the dangerous glaciers of South Georgia Island to the whaling station at Grytviken Harbor with one climbing rope and a single ice axe. Seafarers are still hard put to imagine the difficulties of navigating a 23-foot lifeboat across what Shackleton himself called "the most tempestuous water in the world." Spiritual philosophers still ponder the significance of

Shackleton's remark that during their perilous journey he and his mates seemed accompanied by an unseen and holy presence.

Not surprisingly, the Shackleton family motto is "By Endurance We Conquer," *Fortitudine Vincimus.* One of ten children, Ernest Shackleton was born in Ireland during the great potato famine of 1874. Shackleton's mother, Henrietta Letitia Sophia Gavin, was Irish; his father's ancestors, however, originally came from Yorkshire, England, but moved to County Kildare in the nineteenth century. At the age of thirty-three, Shackleton's father, Henry Shackleton, sensed the catastrophe that might befall his family if he remained a farmer, so gave up agriculture to pursue medicine. In 1884 the family moved to England, where Shackleton would go on to be schooled at Fir Lodge Preparatory School and Dulwich College (where the *James Caird,* the lifeboat that carried Shackleton and his men to eventual safety, is still on display). Shackleton's mother became ill on the move to England and suffered as an invalid for the next forty years of her life. Seven years after moving to London, Shackleton defied his father's wishes that he too pursue medicine, and instead he apprenticed to the merchant marine. Historians would later say that this career choice set Shackleton apart in a positive way from his rival to be, Antarctic explorer Robert Falcon Scott, who was schooled in the ways and mores of the British Navy. Shackleton's career in the merchant marine took him all over the world, as he captained ships that carried mail from England to South Africa, ships that would later carry soldiers to the Cape during the Boer War. He met his wife to be, Emily Dorman, one of his sister's friends, in 1897, married her in 1904, and in 1905 became father of the first of their three children: Raymond, Cecily, and Edward.

During Shackleton's era Antarctica was a tabula rasa, a blank slate at the bottom of the world—a land yet to be explored and mapped, a land not officially owned or governed by any nation. The continent has always been a little-known land that has entranced explorers for centuries. *Terra Australis Incognita,* the unknown southern land, is what the Greeks first called it, then only guessing at its existence. Captain James Cook sailed around the Antarctic Circle in the eighteenth century without ever proving the continent existed. It wasn't until well into the nineteenth century, when whalers ventured further and further south in search of prey, that the continent finally was confirmed as real. The metaphorical possibilities of Antarctica's whiteness, its newness, were clear to Shackleton and other early explorers, who vied to be the first to write upon the fresh page of Antarctica. They wanted, by brilliance, by technology, by sheer will, to make their mark, to extract riches, to make claims in honor of their nations, to test themselves against the ferociousness and mystery of the land, against the very idea of the unknown.

What brought Shackleton to the wild white wilderness of Antarctica was a dream. He responded once to a journalist who asked what inspired him to be an explorer by saying that it had, literally, been a dream that he had had when he was twenty-two years old and aboard his first merchant marine vessel: "We were beating out to New York from Gibraltar, and I dreamt I was standing on the bridge in mid-Atlantic and looking northward. It was a simple dream. I seemed to vow to myself that some day I would go to the region of ice and snow and go on and on till I came to one of the poles of the earth, the end of the axis upon which this great round ball turns." Asked on a different occasion why he continued to return to the Antarctic, Shackleton replied: "I go exploring because I like it and it's my job. One goes once and then gets the fever and can't stop going." He could not, he said, escape "the little voices" that called him to the white south. After his first child was born, he wrote of his eagerness to return to Antarctica: "What I would not give to be out there again doing the job, and this time really on the road to the Pole." He was a man of imagination and determination and had Antarctica in his blood. "I have ideals," Shackleton said, "and far way in my own white south I open my arms to the romance of it all."

Ernest Shackleton was a member of four expeditions to Antarctica: Robert Falcon Scott's 1901–1904 Discovery Expedition; the 1907–1909 Nimrod Expedition; the 1914–1917 Imperial Trans-Antarctic Expedition; and the 1921 Shackleton-Rowett Expedition aboard the *Quest*, from which Shackleton did not return, suffering a massive heart attack while the ship was docked at South Georgia Island. While none of the expeditions met their ultimate goals—to reach the South Pole, to cross the icy continent from one side to the other, or, in the case of the *Quest*, to map the southern coastline of Antarctica—Shackleton is nevertheless hailed as a man who came away from these encounters with The Great White South a heroic success, largely due to his demonstrations of excellent leadership. Shackleton cleverly balanced individuals' strengths and weaknesses to create a stronger whole. His men admired and respected him. "My opinion," said Frank Wild, who served with all of the British explorers in Antarctica, "is that for qualities of leadership, ability to organize, courage in the face of danger, and resource in the overcoming of difficulties, Shackleton stands foremost and must be ranked as the first explorer of his age."

It was in 1901, before his marriage to Emily, when Shackleton first went to Antarctica as third officer on Scott's ship *Discovery*. He was so keen to join the National Antarctic Expedition that he exerted influence, through a friend, upon the expedition's major backer, whom he asked to put in a good word on his behalf. Scott would go on to lead members of the Discovery Expedition, including himself, Shackleton, and Edward Wilson, to 82 degrees south, closer to the South Pole than any humans had been in history. Scurvy and snow blindness, however, kept all three men from reaching the Pole. By February 3, the three had made it back to their ship in McMurdo Sound, but Shackleton was sent home to recover while the *Discovery* stayed one more winter in the Antarctic. It was after this expedition that the historic rivalry between Scott and Shackleton began to take shape; some scholars suggest that being invalided home sparked a competitive spirit in Shackleton. He vowed to return to the ice to prove that he was "a better man than Scott."

During the winter of his first foray in Antarctica, Shackleton lived with the other members of the expedition aboard the ship *Discovery* in Winter Quarters Bay, now the port for the modern United States base at McMurdo Station. It was there that Shackleton edited the very first Antarctic publication, *The South Polar Times*, a proper monthly newspaper, for the edification and amusement of the expedition members, along with a humorous and less intellectual publication called *The Blizzard*.

Shackleton secured funding for his second trip to Antarctica—his own expedition—in 1907. The Nimrod Expedition was based at Cape

Royds, now a weather-beaten hut set amidst the noisy chaos of an Adelie penguin colony about two hours by tracked vehicle from McMurdo Station and Discovery Point, where Shackleton had been based on his earlier trip with Scott. On this expedition Shackleton and three companions would get to within ninety miles of the Pole—a new "farthest South"—but not the coveted southern axis of planet Earth. Instead of pushing on to the Pole when he and his men were exhausted and starving, Shackleton turned around, a surprising move that some call one of the most heroic and best decisions in polar exploration. Shackleton wrote in his diary of that decision: "I cannot think of failure yet. I must look at the matter sensibly and consider the lives of those who are with me . . . man can only do his best. . . ." They safely returned to Cape Royds after having walked 1,700 miles. The new "farthest South" record won Shackleton knighthood in 1909.

The hut at Cape Royds still retains evidence of that winter, when Shackleton and his men, among other activities, printed the first book ever to be published in Antarctica—*Aurora Australis*, an illustrated collection of essays, stories, poems, and musings. No more than thirty copies of the book were made in that little wind-blown hut on the ice —one book for each expedition member. The original volumes were bound with twine into covers of plywood packing cases and sealskin. The books, which are now the prized possessions of family members, friends, museums, and research centers such as the Scott Polar Research Institute in Cambridge, England, are classified as the "Bottled Fruit" copy, or "Irish Stew" copy, based on the label from the packing case still evident on their covers. In his preface to the original *Aurora Australis*, Shackleton wrote: "Some six years ago it fell to my lot to edit and print the first Antarctic publication; it is my fortune now to edit another. . . . During the sunless months which are now our portion; months lit only by vagrant moon and elusive aurora; we have found in this work an interest and a relaxation, and hope eventually it will prove the same to our friends in the distant Northland." The contributions to the volume are signed with pen names, but it is supposed that Shackleton, as "Nemo," wrote the pieces "Midwinter Night" and "Erebus." "Midwinter Night" is a humorous poem that explores, from the point of view of the night watchman, the fantasies, nightmares, and dreams of the "fourteen sleepers," who are his hut-mates. One stanza reads:

> . . . The revels of Eros and Bacchus
> Are mingled in some of their dreams,
> For the songs they gustily gurgle
> Are allied to bibulous themes. . .

The British press loved Shackleton, and upon his return from this second trip, celebrated him as a hero. The government granted him twenty thousand pounds to help pay the expedition's costs, and he began planning for his third and most famous expedition—the Imperial Trans-Antarctic Expedition, which he claimed would be "The greatest Polar journey ever attempted." So eager were the young men of Britain to join him that in 1914 Shackleton collected five thousand applications for only fifty-six spots. At the same historical moment, World War I was beginning to smolder in Europe. Shackleton offered up his men to the British government, but was told by the British Admiralty to "Proceed."

Shackleton's motivation for the Imperial Trans-Antarctic journey came after Norwegian explorer Roald Amundsen planted Norway's flag at the South Pole in 1911, arriving there on December 14, only weeks before Scott reached the Pole with expedition-mates Edward Wilson, Birdie Bowers, Edgar Evans, and Lawrence Oates on January 18, 1912. The Pole had been conquered. Scott had perished. Shackleton vowed that the next great and necessary expedition in the Antarctic would be to cross the continent, from the Weddell Sea across the polar plateau to the Ross Sea.

South, the story of that last great journey, was published in 1919, partly in an attempt to raise funds to pay off the expedition's debts. Between 1919 and 1920, Shackleton lectured daily in London, providing commentary for the silent film footage shot by expedition photographer Frank Hurley. *South* reportedly sold well, although Shackleton himself realized no monetary gain since all the proceeds went to pay debts. The lecturing was boring work and seemed not to capture the popular imagination quite so grandly as Scott's heroic tragedy in 1912. Critics, however, generally responded well to *South*. Apsley Cherry-Garrard, who reviewed the book, praised both it and its author, sticking up for Shackleton against charges that he was a failure because he never, like Scott, reached the Pole:

> Do not let it be said that Shackleton has failed. . . . No man fails who sets an example of high courage, of unbroken resolution, of unshrinking endurance. Explorers run each other down like the deuce. As I read with a critical eye Shackleton's account of the loss of the *Endurance* I get the feeling that he . . . is a good man to get you out of a tight place. There is an impression of the right thing being done without fuss or panic. I know why it is that every man who has served under Shackleton swears by him.

Three years after the publication of *South*, Shackleton sailed for Antarctica again, aboard the *Quest*. He died en route at the age of forty-eight, apparently from heart failure, brought on by years of untreated heart disease, heavy smoking, drinking, and eating. His grave is on South Georgia Island, a place his wife, Emily, said she would rather see him buried—in the wild lands he loved so much rather than in a prim and proper British cemetery. He had once written to her of his longing for the wild: "Sometimes I think I am no good at anything but being away in the wilds with just men."

One of the things that inspires us today about Shackleton and his men, particularly the journey of the *Endurance*, is how they did so much with so little—how they survived with almost no food or equipment amid some of the most brutal natural forces known. For those of us alive at the dawn of the twenty-first century, for whom unexplored lands seem as distant as the moon, for whom technology seems at times to have all the answers, Shackleton's story restores our own faith in the indomitable human spirit. There is something left, it seems, that cannot be bought or sold, that cannot be got through science or technology or money—and that is the mysterious power of the human will. It is hard to know, of course, who Shackleton was, what he thought, what really motivated him, but one impression is that of a fierce but likeable man who wasn't perfect—a man who drank too much and had extramarital affairs, a man friends and foes alike sometimes thought of as a bulldog, in looks and temperament. Perhaps most of all, he was a man that one knew one could count on. Apsley Cherry-Garrard, again sticking up for "The Boss," summed up Shackleton in these famous words: "For a joint scientific and geographical piece of organization, give me Scott; for a Winter Journey, Wilson; for a dash to the Pole and nothing else, Amundsen; and if I am in the devil of a hole and want to get out of it, give me Shackleton every time."

Gretchen Legler is a professor in the Department of Humanities at the University of Maine at Farmington. She is the author of *On the Ice: An Intimate Portrait of Life at McMurdo Station, Antarctica*, a book she researched in Antarctica, where she lived for four months as a fellow in the U.S. National Science Foundation Artists and Writers Program.

SIR ERNEST HENRY SHACKLETON

BOARN IN KILKEE, IRELAND, IN 1874, SON OF HENRY SHACKLETON WHO was of North of England Quaker stock. Educated at Dulwich College 1887 90. He was a junior officer on Scott's Antarctic expedition in the *Discovery* in 1901 and he accompanied Scott on the sledge journey over Ross Shelf Ice. From 1904–5 he was Secretary of the Royal Geographical Society and in 1906 stood unsuccessfully as liberal-unionist candidate for Dundee. In 1907 he sailed in *Nimrod* in command of an expedition which reached a point about 97 miles from the South Pole (1909) and which sent parties to the summit of Mt. Erebus and to the South Magnetic Pole. He described this expedition in *Heart of the Antarctic*. In 1909 he was knighted. Shackleton's trans-Antarctic expedition in the *Endurance* is described in *South,* a classic among books of exploration. He sailed from Plymouth in August 1914, immediately after the outbreak of the war, and for two years the members of the expedition were unaware of the events taking place in the world outside Antarctica. The ordeals that they underwent when the *Endurance* was crushed in the ice and their subsequent tribulations and disappointments make for a story which amply demonstrates the extraordinary determination characterizing those who seek to expand man's horizons.

Always at his best in time of crisis, Shackleton made a voyage of nearly 800 miles in a 22 ft. boat to reach South Georgia and so bring help to the party stranded on Elephant Island. He then rescued those who had gone in the *Aurora* to the Ross Sea in order to meet the trans-polar party.

Shackleton spent the winter of 1918–19 with the North Russian expeditionary force organizing the winter equipment. He died at South Georgia Island in 1922 while on his third expedition to the Antarctic.

Shackleton adopted a new technique of sledge travel and abandoned many of the old traditions of polar exploration. He contributed greatly to geographic and scientific knowledge of Antarctica and though he failed in his attempt to cross the Antarctic continent, it should be remembered that this was not successfully accomplished until 1958 by the party led by Sir Vivian Fuchs.

PREFACE

AFTER THE CONQUEST OF THE SOUTH POLE BY AMUNDSEN, WHO, BY A narrow margin of days, was in advance of the British expedition under Scott, only one great main object of Antarctic journeyings remained—the crossing of the South Polar continent from sea to sea.

After hearing of Amundsen's success, I began to make preparations to start a last great journey, so that the first crossing of the last continent should be achieved by a British expedition.

We failed in this object, but the story of our attempt is the subject of the following pages, and I think, although failure in the actual accomplishment must be recorded, that there are chapters in this book of high adventure, unique experiences, and, above all, records of unflinching determination, supreme loyalty and generous self-sacrifice on the part of my men, which will appeal urgently to everyone who is interested in the tale of the White Warfare of the South.

The struggles, disappointments and endurance of this small party of Britishers, hidden for nearly two years in the fastnesses of the Polar ice, make a story which is unique in the history of Antarctic exploration.

Owing to the loss of the *Endurance* and the disaster to the *Aurora*, documents relating mainly to the organization and preparation of the expedition have been lost, but I will insert here a part of the program which I prepared in order to arouse the interest of the public in the expedition.

THE TRANS-CONTINENTAL PARTY

The first crossing of the Antarctic continent, from sea to sea, via the Pole, apart from its historic value, will be a journey of great scientific importance.

The distance will be roughly 1,800 miles, and the first half of this, from the Weddell Sea to the Pole, will be over unknown ground. Every step will be an advance in geographical science. It will be learned whether the great Victoria chain of mountains, which has been traced from the Ross Sea to the Pole, extends across the continent and thus links up (except for the ocean break) with the Andes of South America, and whether the great plateau around the Pole dips gradually towards the Weddell Sea.

Continuous magnetic observations will be taken on the journey. Meteorological conditions will be noted carefully, and ice formations and the nature of the mountains will be studied.

SCIENTIFIC WORK BY OTHER PARTIES

While the trans-continental party is carrying out, for the British flag, the greatest Polar journey ever attempted, the other parties will be engaged in important scientific work.

Two sledging parties will operate from the base on the Weddell Sea. One will travel westwards towards Graham Land, collecting geological specimens, and proving whether there are mountains in that region linked up with those found on the other side of the Pole.

Another party will travel eastward toward Enderby Land, and a third, remaining at the base, will study the fauna of the land and sea, and the meteorological conditions.

From the Ross Sea base, on the other side of the Pole,. another party will push southward, and probably will await the arrival of the trans-continental party at the top of the Beardmore Glacier, near Mount Buckley, a region of great importance to the geologist.

Both the ships of the expedition will be fully equipped for scientific work. The Weddell Sea ship will try to trace the unknown coastline of Graham Land.

The several shore parties and the two ships will thus carry out geographical and scientific work on a scale and over an area never before attempted by one Polar expedition.

This will be the first use of the Weddell Sea as a base for exploration, and all the parties will open up vast stretches of unknown land. It is appropriate that this work should be carried out under the British flag, since the whole of the area southward to the Pole is British territory.

HOW THE CONTINENT WILL BE CROSSED

The Weddell Sea ship, with all the members of the expedition operating from that base, will leave Buenos Aires in October 1914 and try to land in November in latitude 78 degrees south. Should this be done, the trans-continental party will start immediately on their 1,800-mile journey, in the hope of accomplishing the march across the Pole and reaching the Ross Sea base in five months. Should the landing be made too late in the season, the party will go into winter quarters, and as early as possible in 1915 set out on the journey.

The trans-continental party will be led by Sir Ernest Shackleton, and will consist of six men. The equipment will embody everything that the experience of the leader and his expert advisers can suggest. When this party has reached the area of the Pole, after covering 800 miles of unknown ground, it will strike due north towards the head of the Beardmore Glacier, and there it is hoped to meet the outcoming party from the Ross Sea. Both will join up and make for the Ross Sea base.

In all, fourteen men will be landed by the *Endurance* on the Weddell Sea. Six will set out on the trans-continental journey, three will go westward, three eastward, and two will remain at the base.

The *Aurora* will land six men at the Ross Sea base. They will lay down depots on the route of the trans-continental party and make a march south to assist that party.

Should the trans-continental party succeed in crossing during the first season, its return to civilization may be expected about April 1915. The other sections in April 1916.

THE SHIPS OF THE EXPEDITION

The two ships have been selected.

The *Endurance*, which will take the trans-continental party to the Weddell Sea, and will afterwards explore along an unknown coastline, is a new vessel, specially constructed for Polar work under the supervision of a committee of Polar explorers. To enable her to stay longer at sea, she will carry oil fuel as well as coal. She is of about 350 tons, and this fine vessel, equipped, has cost the expedition £14,000.

The *Aurora*, which will take out the Ross Sea party, has been bought from Dr. Mawson. She is similar in all respects to the *Terra Nova*, of Captain Scott's last expedition. She is now at Hobart, Tasmania, where the Ross Sea party will join her in October next.

I started the preparations in the middle of 1913, but no public announcement was made until January 13th, 1914, and the first result of this was a flood of applications from all classes of the community to join the adventure. I received nearly five thousand applications, and from these I picked fifty-six men.

In March, to my great anxiety, I was disappointed in the financial help which had been promised me, and was faced with the fact that I had contracted for a ship and stores, and had engaged the staff, and was not in possession of funds to meet these liabilities.

I immediately began to appeal for help, and met with generous response from all sides. It is impossible to mention everyone who supported my application, but I must particularly refer to a munificent gift of £24,000 from the late Sir James Caird, and to one of £10,000 from the British government. I wish also especially to thank Mr. Dudley Docker, Miss Elizabeth Dawson Lambton, Dame Janet Stancomb Wills, and the Royal Geographical Society, for their generosity.

The only return and privilege an explorer has in the way of acknowledgment for the help given to him is to record on the discovered lands the names of those to whom the expedition owes its being. I have the honor to place on the new land the names of the above and of other generous contributors to the expedition.

So the equipment and organization of the expedition went on, until towards the end of July everything was ready. And then the war clouds suddenly darkened over Europe.

It had been arranged for the *Endurance* to proceed to Cowes to be inspected by His Majesty, but I received a message to say that the King would be unable to go to Cowes.

We sailed from London on Friday, August 1st, 1914, and anchored off Southend for the whole of Saturday. Growing hourly more anxious as the rumors spread, I took the ship to Margate on Sunday afternoon; and on Monday morning I went ashore, and in the morning paper I read the order for general mobilization.

I immediately returned to the ship, and, having mustered all hands, I told them that I proposed to send a telegram to the Admiralty offering the ship, stores, and, if they agreed, our own services in the event of war. Our only request was that, if war broke out, the expedition might be considered as a single unit, for there were enough trained and experienced men among us to man a destroyer. Within an hour I received a laconic wire from the Admiralty saying "Proceed." A little later Mr. Winston Churchill wired thanking us for our offer, and saying that the authorities desired that the expedition should go on.

Following these definite instructions, the *Endurance* sailed to Plymouth, and on the Tuesday the King sent for me and handed me the Union Jack to carry on the expedition. On that night, at midnight, war was declared.

On the following Saturday, August 8th, the *Endurance* sailed from Plymouth, obeying the direct orders of the Admiralty.

I make particular reference to this phase of the expedition, as there was a certain amount of criticism of the expedition having left the country. Concerning this criticism I wish to say that our preparations had been going on for over a year, that large sums of money had been spent, that we offered to give up the expedition without even consulting the donors of this money, and that few people imagined at this time that the war would last for years and involve nearly the whole world.

The expedition was going to a most dangerous and strenuous work, which has nearly always caused a certain percentage of loss of life. Finally, when the expedition did return, practically all the members who had passed unscathed through the dangers of the Antarctic took their places in the wider field of battle, and the percentage of casualties among them was high.

The voyage to Buenos Aires was uneventful, and on October 26th we sailed from there for South Georgia, the most southerly outpost of the British Empire. Here, for a month, we were engaged in final preparations.

Apart from private individuals and societies, I wish also most gratefully to acknowledge the assistance rendered by the Dominion government of New Zealand, the Commonwealth government of Australia, the Uruguayan government, and the Chilean government, which was directly responsible for the rescue of my comrades.

ERNEST SHACKLETON

CHAPTER ONE

INTO THE WEDDELL SEA

I HAD DECIDED TO LEAVE SOUTH GEORGIA ABOUT DECEMBER 5th, 1914, and in the intervals of final preparation I scanned again the plans for the voyage to winter quarters. What welcome was the Weddell Sea preparing for us?

Following the advice of the whaling captains at South Georgia, who generously placed their knowledge at my disposal, I had decided to steer to the South Sandwich Group, round Ultima Thule, and work as far to the eastward as the fifteenth meridian west longitude before pushing south. The whalers warned me of the difficulty of getting through the ice in the neighborhood of the South Sandwich Group, and they thought that the expedition would have to push through heavy pack in order to reach the Weddell Sea. Probably the best time to get into the Weddell Sea would be about the end of February. Owing to the warnings of the whalers I decided to take the deck-load of coal, for if we had to fight our way through to Coats' Land we should need all the fuel we could carry.

At length the day of departure arrived. I gave the order to heave anchor at 8:45 AM on December 5th, and the clanking of the windlass broke for us the last link with civilization. The morning was dull and overcast, but hearts aboard the *Endurance* were light. The long days of preparation were over and the adventure lay ahead.

The wind freshened during the day and all square sail was set, with the foresail reefed in order to give the lookout a clear view ahead, for we did not wish to risk contact with a "growler," one of those treacherous fragments of ice that float with surface awash. During December 6th we made good progress on a southeasterly course, but December 7th brought the first check. At six o'clock on that morning the sea, which had been green in color on the previous day, changed suddenly to a deep indigo.

Sanders Island and Candlemas were sighted early in the afternoon, and large numbers of bergs, mostly tabular in form, lay to the west of the islands. The presence of so many bergs was ominous, and immediately after passing between the islands we encountered stream-ice. All sail was taken in and we proceeded slowly under steam. At 8 PM the *Endurance* was confronted by a belt of heavy pack-ice, half a mile broad and extending north and south. There was clear water beyond, but the pack in our neighborhood was impenetrable. This was disconcerting. The noon latitude had been 57° 26' S., and I had not expected to find pack-ice nearly so far north.

During that night the situation became dangerous. We pushed into the pack in the hope of reaching open water beyond, and found ourselves in a pool which was growing smaller and smaller. Worsley and I were on deck all night, dodging the pack, but some anxious hours passed before we rounded it and were able to set sail once more.

This initial tussle with the pack had been exciting. Pieces of ice and bergs of all sizes were heaving and jostling against each other in the heavy southwesterly swell. In spite of all our care the *Endurance* struck large lumps stern on, but the engines were stopped in time and no harm was done.

During December 9th we again encountered the pack, and after rounding it we steered S. 40° E., and at noon on the 10th we reached lat. 58° 28' S., long. 20° 28' W. On the following day we met with loose pack which did not present great difficulties. Worsley, Wild and I, with three officers, kept three watches while we were working through the pack, so that we had two officers on deck all the time. The carpenter had rigged a six-foot wooden semaphore on the bridge to enable the navigating officer to give the seamen or scientists at the wheel the direction and the exact amount of helm required. This device saved time as well as the effort of shouting.

During December 12 and 13 we made fair progress, but on the 14 conditions became more difficult, for the pack was denser than it had been on the previous days. The most careful navigation could not prevent an occasional bump against ice too thick to be broken or pushed aside, but although the propeller received several blows no damage was done. During the afternoon of the 14 a southwesterly gale sprang up, and at 8 PM we hove to, stem against a floe, it being impossible to proceed without serious risk of damaging the rudder or propeller.

The *Endurance* remained against the floe for the next twenty-four hours, when the gale moderated. The pack extended to the horizon in all directions and was broken by innumerable narrow lanes. We made five miles to the south before midnight, and we continued to advance until 4 AM on December 17, when the ice once more became difficult. Very large floes of six-months-old ice lay close together, and some of these floes presented a square mile of unbroken surface.

The morning of December 18 found the *Endurance* proceeding amongst large floes with thin ice between them, and shortly before noon further progress was barred by heavy pack, and we put an ice-anchor on the floe and banked the fires.

I had been prepared for evil conditions in the Weddell Sea, but had hoped that in December and January the pack would be loose, even if no open water was to be found. What we were encountering was fairly dense pack of a very obstinate character.

Pack-ice may be described as a gigantic and interminable jigsaw puzzle devised by nature. The parts of the puzzle in loose pack have floated slightly apart and become disarranged; at numerous places they have pressed together again; as the pack gets closer the congested areas grow larger and the parts are jammed harder until it becomes "close pack"; then the whole jigsaw puzzle becomes so jammed that with care it can be crossed in every direction on foot. Where the parts do not fit closely there is, of course, open water, which freezes over in a few hours after giving off volumes of "frost-smoke." In obedience to renewed pressure this young ice "rafts," thus forming double thicknesses of toffee-like consistency.

All through the winter the drifting pack changes—grows by freezing, thickens by rafting, and corrugates by pressure. If, finally, in its drift it impinges on a coast, such as the western shore of the Weddell Sea, terrific pressure is set up and an inferno of ice-blocks, ridges and hedgerows results, extending possibly for 150 or 200 miles offshore.

I have given this explanation so that the nature of the ice through which we had to push our way for hundreds of miles may be understood.

The conditions did not improve during December 19th, and after proceeding for two hours the *Endurance* was stopped again by heavy floes, and, owing to a heavy gale, we remained moored to a floe during the following day. The members of the staff and crew took advantage of the pause to enjoy a vigorous game of football on the level surface of the floe alongside the ship.

Monday, December 21st, was beautifully fine, and we made an early start through the pack. Petrels of several species, penguins and seals were plentiful, and we saw four small blue whales. At noon we entered a long lead to the southward and passed nine splendid bergs. One huge specimen was shaped like the Rock of Gibraltar but with steeper cliffs, and another had a natural dock which would have contained the *Aquitania*. Hurley brought out his kinematograph-camera to make a record of these bergs. We found long leads during the afternoon, but at midnight the ship was stopped by small, heavy ice-floes, tightly packed against an unbroken plain of ice. The outlook from the mast-head was not encouraging; the big floe was at least fifteen miles long and ten miles wide. I had never seen such an area of unbroken ice in the Ross Sea.

We waited with banked fires for an opportunity to proceed, and during the evening of December 22nd some lanes opened, and we were able again to move towards the south. So we struggled on until Christmas Day, when we were held up by more bad weather. However, we had a really splendid dinner, and in the evening everybody joined in a "sing-song."

The weather was still bad on December 26th and 27th, but on the evening of December 29th the high winds which had prevailed for four and a half days gave way to a gentle southerly breeze, and when the New Year dawned we had pushed and fought the little ship 480 miles through loose and close pack-ice. Our advance through the pack had been in a S. 10° E. direction, and I estimated that the total steaming distance had exceeded 700 miles.

The first hundred miles had been through loose pack, but the greatest hindrances had been the southwesterly gales. The last 250 miles had been through close pack alternating with fine long leads and stretches of open water.

CHAPTER TWO

New Land

THE CONDITION OF THE PACK IMPROVED IN THE EVENING OF NEW Year's Day, and we progressed rapidly until a moderate gale came up from the east, with continuous snow. Early in the morning of January 2nd we got into thick old pack-ice. The position then was lat. 69° 49' S., long. 15° 42' W., and the run for the last twenty-four hours had been 124 miles S. 3° W., which was cheering.

This good run had made me hopeful of sighting the land on the following day, but we were delayed by heavy pack and also by the gale. I was becoming anxious to reach land on account of the dogs, with which I had been greatly pleased when we had started, but, owing to lack of exercise, they were now becoming run-down.

Difficulties continued to beset us, and on the 4th we had been steaming and dodging about over an area of twenty square miles for fifty hours, trying to find an opening to the south, southeast, or southwest, but all the leads ran north, northeast, or northwest. It was as if the spirits of the Antarctic were pointing us to the backward track—the track we were determined not to follow.

Our desire was to make easting as well as southing, so that, if possible, we might reach the land east of Ross' farthest south, and well east of Coats' Land.

Solid pack, however, barred the way to the south, but on the 6th, with the ship moored to a floe, I took the opportunity to exercise the dogs. Their excitement when they got on to the floe was intense;

several of them managed to get into the water, and their muzzles did not prevent them from having some hot fights. On the following day, when we were able to make some progress, killer whales began to be active around us, and I had to exercise caution in allowing anyone to leave the ship. These beasts have a habit of locating a resting seal by looking over the edge of a floe, and then striking through the ice from below in search of a meal; they would not distinguish between seal and man.

On the 8th and 9th fortune was with us, and the run southward in blue water, with a path clear ahead and the miles falling away behind us, was a joyful experience after the long struggle through the ice lanes; but, like other good things, our spell of free movement had to end, and the *Endurance* encountered the ice again at 1 AM on the 10th.

At noon our position was lat. 72° 02′ S., long. 16° 07′ W., and we were now near the land discovered by Dr. W. S. Bruce, leader of the *Scotia* expedition, in 1904, and named by him Coats' Land. Dr. Bruce encountered an ice barrier in lat. 72° 18′ S., long. 10° W., and from his description of rising slopes of snow and ice, with shoaling water off the barrier-wall, the presence of land was clearly indicated. It was up those slopes, at a point as far south as possible, that I planned to begin the march across the Antarctic continent. All hands now were watching for the coast described by Dr. Bruce, and at 5 PM the lookout reported an appearance of land to the south-southeast. It seemed to be an island or a peninsula with a sound on its south side. At the time we were passing through heavy loose pack, and shortly before midnight we broke into a lead of open sea along a barrier edge. The barrier was 70 feet high with cliffs of about 40 feet, and the *Scotia* must have passed this point when pushing to Bruce's farthest south on March 6th, 1904.

Thick and overcast weather impeded our progress on the following days, but on the 12th we were beyond the point reached by the *Scotia,* and the land underlying the ice sheet, which we were skirting, was new. At 4 PM on the 13th, when we were still following the barrier to the southwest, we reached a corner and found it receding abruptly to the southeast. Our way was blocked by very heavy pack, and as we were unable to find an opening we moored the ship to a floe and banked fires.

Several young emperor penguins had been captured and brought aboard on the previous day, and two of them were still alive when the *Endurance* was brought alongside the floe. They promptly hopped on to the ice, turned round, bowed gracefully three times, and retired to the far side of the floe. There is something curiously human about the manners and movements of these birds. I was again concerned about the dogs. Some of them appeared to be ailing, and one dog had to be shot on the 12th.

We did not move the ship on the 14th, but on the following day conditions had improved, and in the evening the *Endurance* was moving southward with sails set and we continued to skirt the barrier in clear weather. I was watching for possible landing places, though, as a matter of fact, unless compelled by necessity, I had no intention of landing north of Vahsel Bay, in Luitpold Land. Every mile gained towards the south meant a mile less sledging when the time came for the overland journey.

Shortly before midnight on the 15th we came abreast of the northern edge of a great glacier, projecting beyond the barrier into the sea. It was about 400 ft. high, and at its edge was a large mass of thick bay-ice. The bay formed by the northern edge of this glacier would have made an excellent landing place, for it was protected from the south-easterly wind and was open only to a northerly wind. I named the place Glacier Bay, and had reason later to remember it with regret.

The *Endurance* steamed along the front of this glacier for about seventeen miles, and at 4 AM on the 16th we reached the edge of another huge glacial overflow from the ice sheet. We steamed along the front of this tremendous glacier for forty miles and then were held up by solid pack-ice, which appeared to be held by stranded bergs. No further advance was possible for that day, but the noon observation showed that we had gained 124 miles to the southwest during the preceding twenty-four hours. We pushed the ship against a small berg, and a blizzard from the east-northeast prevented us from leaving the shelter of the berg on the following day (Sunday, January 17th).

The land, when the air was clear, seemed to rise to 3000 feet above the head of the glacier. Caird Coast, as I named it, connects Coats' Land, discovered by Bruce in 1904, with Luitpold Land, discovered by Filchner in 1912. We were now close to the junction with Luitpold Land.

The ship lay under the lee of the stranded berg until 7 AM on January 18th, by which time the gale had moderated so much that we could sail to the southwest through a lane which had opened along the glacier front, and on the morning of the 19th our position was lat. 76° 34′ S., long. 31° 30′ W. The weather was good, but as the ice had closed around the ship during the night, no advance could be made. A survey of the position on the 20th showed that the *Endurance* was firmly beset. As far as the eye could reach from the masthead the ice was packed heavily and firmly all round the ship in every direction.

Many uneventful days followed. Moderate breezes from the east and southwest had no apparent effect upon the ice, and the ship remained firmly held. On the 27th, the tenth day of inactivity, I decided to let the fires out. We had been burning half a ton of coal a day to keep steam in the boilers, and as the bunkers now contained only sixty-seven tons, representing thirty-three days' steaming, we could not afford this expenditure of coal.

During these days of waiting we gradually collected a stock of seal meat, which the dogs needed, and which also made a very welcome change from our rations.

Not until February 9th did I order steam to be raised in the hope of being able to proceed, but our effort failed. We could break the young ice, but the pack defied us and the ship became jammed against soft floe. As there seemed small chance of making a move, I had the motor crawler and warper put on the floe for a trial run. The motor worked most successfully, running at about six miles an hour over slabs and ridges of ice hidden by a foot or two of soft snow. The surface was worse than we should have expected to face on land or barrier-ice.

No important change in our situation took place during the second part of February. Early in the morning of the 14th I ordered a good head of steam on the engines and sent all hands on to the floe with ice-chisels, prickers, saws and picks. All that day and most of the next we worked strenuously to get the ship into the lead ahead of us. After terrific labor we got the ship a third of the way to the lead, but about 400 yards of heavy ice still separated the *Endurance* from the water, and reluctantly I was compelled to admit that further effort was useless. Every opening we made froze up again quickly owing to the unseasonably low temperature.

The abandonment of the attack was a great disappointment to all hands. The men had worked so splendidly that they had deserved success, but the task was beyond our powers. I had not yet abandoned hope of getting clear, but by this time I was beginning to count on the possibility of having to spend a winter in the inhospitable arms of the pack. The sun, which had been above the horizon for two months, set at midnight on the 17th, and, although it would not disappear until April, its slanting rays warned us of the approach of winter. We continued to accumulate a supply of seal meat and blubber, and the excursions across the floes to shoot and bring in the seals provided welcome exercise for all hands.

On the 22nd the *Endurance* reached the farthest south point of her drift, touching the 77th parallel of latitude in long. 35° W. The summer had gone; indeed, it had scarcely been with us at all. The temperatures were very low both day and night, and as the pack was freezing solidly around the ship, I could no longer doubt that the *Endurance* was confined for the winter.

"We must," I wrote,

> . . . wait for the spring, which may bring us better fortune. If I had guessed a month ago that the ice would grip us here, I would have established our base at one of the landing places at the great glacier. But there seemed no reason to anticipate then that the fates would prove unkind. . . . My chief anxiety is the drift. Where will the vagrant winds and currents carry the ship during the long winter months that are ahead of us? We will go west, no doubt, but how far? And will it be possible to break out of the pack early in the spring and reach Vahsel Bay or some other suitable landing place? These are momentous questions for us.

On February 24th we ceased to observe ship routine, and the *Endurance* became a winter station. Orders were given for the after-hold to be cleared and the stores checked so that we might know exactly how we stood for a siege by an Antarctic winter. The dogs went off the ship on the following day, their kennels being placed on the floe along the length of a wire rope to which the leashes were fastened. They were obviously delighted to get off the ship, and we had already begun the training of teams. Hockey and football on the floe were our chief recreations, and all hands joined in many a strenuous game. We kept our wireless apparatus rigged, but without result. Evidently the distances were too great for our small plant.

CHAPTER THREE

Winter Months

MARCH OPENED WITH A SEVERE NORTHEASTERLY GALE WHICH LASTED until the 3rd. All hands were employed in clearing out the 'tween-decks, which was to be converted into a living room and dining room for officers and scientists. Here the carpenter erected the stove that had been intended for the shore hut, and the quarters were made very snug. The dogs seemed indifferent to the blizzard, and were content to lie most of the time curled into tight balls under the snow.

When the gale cleared we found that the pack had been driven in from the northeast and was more firmly consolidated than before. A new berg, probably fifteen miles in length, appeared on the northern horizon, and the sighting of it was of more than passing interest, since in that comparatively shallow sea it was possible for a big berg to become stranded. Then the island of ice would be a center of tremendous pressure and disturbance amid the drifting pack. We had seen something already of the smashing effect of a contest between berg and floe, and did not wish to see the helpless *Endurance* involved in such a battle of giants.

The quarters in the 'tween-decks were completed by the 10th, and the men took possession of the cubicles which had been built. The largest cubicle contained Macklin, McIlroy, Hurley and Hussey; Clark and Wordie lived opposite in a room called "Auld Reekie." Next came the abode of "The Nuts," or engineers, followed by "The Sailors' Rest," which was inhabited by Cheetham and McNeish.

The new quarters became known as "The Ritz," and meals were served there instead of in the wardroom. Wild, Marston, Crean and Worsley established themselves in cubicles in the wardroom, and by the middle of the month all hands had settled down to the winter routine. I lived alone aft.

The noon position on the 14th was lat. 76° 54′ S., long. 36° 10′ W. The land was visible faintly to the southeast, distant about thirty-six miles. The drift of the ship was still towards the northwest. I had the boilers blown down on the 15th, and the consumption of 2 cwt. of coal per day, to keep the boilers from freezing, ceased. Anyhow there would not be much coal left for steaming purposes in the spring, but I hoped to eke out the supply with blubber.

The training of the dogs in sledge teams continued. The orders used by the drivers were "Mush" (go on), "Gee" (right), "Haw" (left), and "Whoa" (stop). These are the words which Canadian drivers adopted long ago, borrowing them originally from England. The teams rapidly became efficient, but we were losing dogs owing to sickness.

As the days passed the sun sank lower in the sky, the temperature became lower, and the *Endurance* felt the grip of the icy hand of winter; but the month of April was not uneventful. During the night of the 3rd we heard the ice grinding to the eastward, and in the morning we saw that young ice was rafted 8 to 10 feet high in places. This was the first murmur of the danger which was so greatly to threaten us in later months. The ice was heard grinding and creaking during the 4th and the ship vibrated slightly. I gave orders that accumulations of snow, ice and rubbish alongside the *Endurance* should be shoveled away, so that in case of pressure there would be no weight against the topsides to check the ship rising above the ice.

Again, on the 9th, there were signs of pressure, and, although the movement was not serious, I realized that it might be the beginning of trouble for the expedition. We brought certain stores aboard, and provided space on deck for the dogs in case they had to be removed at short notice from the floe.

The dogs had been divided into six teams of nine dogs each. Wild, Crean, Macklin, McIlroy, Marston and Hurley each had charge of a team, and were fully responsible for their own dogs. We were still losing dogs, and it was unfortunate that we had not the proper remedies for the disease from which they were suffering. By the end of April our mature dogs had decreased to fifty. Our store of seal meat now amounted to 5,000 lb., and I calculated that we had enough meat and blubber to feed the dogs for ninety days without trenching upon the sledging rations.

On the 14th a new berg, which was destined to give us cause for anxiety, appeared. It was a big berg, and during the day it increased its apparent altitude and slightly changed its bearing. Evidently it was aground and was holding its position against the drifting pack. During the next twenty-four hours the *Endurance* moved steadily towards the berg. We could see from the masthead that the pack was piling and rafting against the mass of ice, and it was easy to imagine the fate of the ship if she entered the area of disturbance. She would be crushed like an eggshell amid the shattering masses.

The drift of the pack was not constant, and during the succeeding days the berg, which was about three-quarters of a mile long on the side presented to us and probably considerably more than 200 feet high, alternately advanced and receded as the *Endurance* moved with the floe. On Sunday, April 18th, it was only seven miles distant from the ship, but a strong drift to the westward during the night of the 18th relieved our anxiety by carrying the *Endurance* to the lee of the berg, and before the end of the month it was no longer in sight.

We said goodbye to the sun on May 1st and entered the period of twilight, which would be followed by the darkness of midwinter. I wrote:

One feels our helplessness as the long winter night closes upon us. By this time, if fortune had smiled upon the expedition, we would have been comfortably and securely established in a shore base, with depots laid to the south, and plans made for the long march in the spring and summer. Where will we make a landing now? . . . Time alone will tell. I do not think any member of the expedition is disheartened by our disappointment. All hands are cheery and busy, and will do their best when the time for acting comes. In the meantime we must wait.

The ship's position on Sunday, May 2nd, was lat. 75° 23' S., long. 42° 14' W., and on that day we captured a seal, which was the first we had caught since March 19th. On the following day three emperor penguins appeared and were captured, and on the same afternoon we sighted five more emperors and secured one of them, Kerr and Cheetham fighting a valiant action against two large birds. Kerr rushed at one of them and seized it, but was promptly knocked down by the angry penguin, which jumped on his chest before retiring. Then Cheetham came to Kerr's assistance, and between them they seized another penguin, and bound his bill and led him, muttering muffled protests, to the ship, the bird looking like an inebriated old man between two policemen. This penguin weighed 85 lb.

On May 4th we secured two more emperors, and while Wordie was leading one of them to the ship Wild came along with his dog team. The dogs, immediately uncontrollable, made a frantic rush for the bird, and were almost upon him when their harness caught on an ice-pylon, which they had tried to pass on both sides at once. The result was a seething tangle of dogs, traces, men and overturned sledge, while the penguin, three yards away, indifferently surveyed the disturbance. During the succeeding days we secured several birds, and they made an important addition to our supply of fresh food.

The month of May passed with few incidents of importance, and the drift of the *Endurance* continued with only occasional reports of pressure during June. The light by now was very bad, except when the friendly moon was above the horizon.

In those days the care of our dog teams was our heaviest responsibility, and a faint twilight round about noon of each day assisted us in the important work of exercising them. Whatever fate might be in store for us the conditioning and training of the dogs seemed essential, and whenever the weather permitted the teams were taken out by their drivers. Rivalries naturally arose, and on the 15th a great race, the "Antarctic Derby," was run. Considerable betting took place, but the most thrilling wagers were those which concerned stores of chocolate and cigarettes.

A course of about 700 yards had been laid out, and five teams went to the starting point in the dim noon twilight, with a zero temperature and an aurora flickering faintly to the southward. Wild's time for the course was 2 minutes 16 seconds, and in a subsequent race against Hurley's team Wild's dogs completed the course in 2 minutes 9 seconds, although their load was 910 lb., or 130 lb. per dog.

The approach of the returning sun was indicated by beautiful sunrise glows on the horizon in the early days of July. By the 10th numerous cracks and leads extended in all directions to within 300 yards of the ship, but although we heard occasional sounds of moderate pressure, the *Endurance* was not involved.

On the evening of the 13th the most severe blizzard we had experienced in the Weddell Sea swept down upon us, and early in the following morning the kennels to the southern side of the ship were buried under 5 feet of drift. The ship was invisible at a distance of 50 yards, and I gave orders that nobody should go beyond the kennels, for it was impossible to preserve a sense of direction in the raging wind and suffocating drift. The temperature during the blizzard ranged from –21° to –33.5° Fahr., and by evening the gale had attained a force of sixty or seventy miles an hour, and the ship was trembling under the attack. We, however, were snug enough in our quarters aboard until the morning of the 14th, when all hands turned out to shovel the snow from deck and kennels. The temperature was then about –30° Fahr., and it was necessary to be on guard against frostbite.

The weather did not clear until the 16th, and then we saw that the appearance of the surrounding pack had been altered completely by the blizzard. The "island" floe containing the *Endurance* still stood fast, but cracks and masses of ice thrown up by pressure could be seen in all directions.

The ice-pressure, which was indicated by distant rumblings and by the appearance of formidable ridges, was now causing us more and more anxiety. The areas of disturbance were gradually approaching the ship. Early on the afternoon of the 22nd a 2-foot crack, running southwest and northeast for a distance of about two miles, approached to within 35 yards of the port quarter.

I had all the sledges brought aboard and set a special watch in case it became necessary hurriedly to get the dogs off the floe. This crack was the result of heavy pressure 300 yards away on the port bow, where

huge blocks of ice were piled up in wild and threatening confusion.
The pressure at that point was enormous; blocks weighing many tons
were raised 15 feet above the level of the floe. I arranged to divide the
night watches with Worsley and Wild, and none of us had much rest.
The ship was shaken by heavy bumps, and we were on the alert to see
that no dogs had fallen into the cracks.

In the morning we saw that our island had been reduced considerably during the night. Our long months of rest and safety seemed to
have ended, and a period of stress to have begun.

During the following day I had a store of sledging provisions, oil,
matches, and other essentials placed on the upper deck handy to the
starboard quarter boat, so that we should be ready for a sudden emergency. A great deal of ice-pressure was heard and observed in all
directions during the 25th, much of it close to the port quarter of the
ship. The floe which held the *Endurance* was swung to and fro by the pressure during the day, but came back to the old bearing before midnight.

At this time I wrote:

The ice for miles around is much looser. There are numerous
cracks and short leads to the northeast and southeast. Ridges
are being forced up in all directions. . . . It would be a relief to
be able to make some effort on our own behalf; but we can do
nothing until the ice releases our ship. If the floes continue to
loosen, we may break out within the next few weeks and resume
the fight. In the meantime the pressure continues, and it is
hard to foresee the outcome. . . . All hands are cheered by the
indication that the end of the winter darkness is near.

The break-up of our floe came suddenly on Sunday, August 1st, just
one year after the *Endurance* left the Southwest India Docks on the voyage to the Far South. The position was lat. 72° 26′ S., long. 48° 10′ W.
The morning brought a moderate southwesterly gale with heavy snow,
and presently, after some warning movements of the ice, the floe
began to break up all round us under pressure, and the ship listed
over 10 degrees to starboard.

I had the dogs and sledges brought aboard at once and the gang-
way hoisted. The dogs seemed to realize their danger and behaved

most peacefully. The pressure was rapidly cracking the floe, rafting it close to the ship and forcing masses of ice beneath the keel. The *Endurance* listed heavily to port against the gale, and, at the same time, was forced ahead, astern and sideways several times by the grinding floes. She received one or two hard nips, but resisted them without as much as a creak.

At one stage it looked as if the ship was to be made the plaything of successive floes, and I was relieved when she came to a standstill with a large piece of our old "dock" under the starboard bilge. I had the boats cleared away ready for lowering, got up some additional stores, and set a double watch. Around us lay the ruins of "Dog Town"; it was a sad sight, but my chief concern just then was about the safety of the rudder, which was being attacked viciously by the ice. I could see that some damage had been done, but it was at the time impossible to make a close examination.

After the ship had come to a standstill in her new position very heavy pressure was set up, but the *Endurance* had been built to withstand the attacks of the ice, and she lifted bravely as the floes drove beneath her. The effects of the pressure around us were awe-inspiring. Mighty blocks of ice, gripped between meeting floes, rose slowly until they jumped like cherry-stones squeezed between thumb and finger. The pressure of millions of tons of moving ice was crushing and smashing inexorably. If the ship was once gripped firmly her fate would be sealed.

By the afternoon of the 2nd the gale had moderated and the pressure had almost ceased. The gale had given us some northing, but it had also severely damaged the rudder of the *Endurance*. Heavy masses of ice were still jammed against the stern, and it was consequently impossible to ascertain the extent of the damage.

The weather on August 3rd was overcast and misty, and on the following day all hands and the carpenter were busy making and placing kennels on the upper deck, and by nightfall the dogs were comfortably housed and ready for any weather. The sun showed through the clouds above the northern horizon for nearly an hour.

The remaining days of August were comparatively uneventful. The ice around the ship again froze firmly and little movement occurred in our neighborhood. The training of the dogs proceeded actively, and we continued to drift steadily to the northwest. Minus temperatures prevailed still, but the daylight was increasing. A sounding on the 17th gave 1,676 fathoms, ten miles west of the charted position of Morell Land. No land could be seen from the masthead, and I decided that Morell Land must be added to the long list of Antarctic islands and continental coasts which on close investigation have resolved themselves into icebergs.

On August 24th we were two miles north of the latitude of Morell's farthest south, and over 10° of longitude, or more than 200 miles, west of his position. There was some movement of the ice near the ship during the last days of the month, and all hands were called out on the night of the 26th, sounds of pressure having been followed by the cracking of the ice alongside the ship; but the trouble did not develop immediately.

I calculated that we were 250 miles from the nearest known land to the westward, and more than 500 miles from the nearest outpost of civilization, Wilhelmina Bay. I hoped fervently that we should not have to undertake a march across the moving ice fields. We knew the *Endurance* to be stout and true, but these were anxious days because no ship ever built by man could live, if taken fairly in the grip of the floes and prevented from rising to the surface of the grinding ice.

→ CHAPTER FOUR ←

LOSS OF THE ENDURANCE

THE ICE DID NOT SERIOUSLY TROUBLE US AGAIN UNTIL THE END OF September, though during the whole month the floes were seldom entirely without movement. The routine of work and play on the *Endurance* steadily proceeded. Our plans and preparations for any contingency which might arise during the approaching summer had been made, but there was always plenty to do in and about our prisoned ship. Runs with the dogs and vigorous games of hockey and football on the rough, snow-covered floe kept all hands in good condition.

By the middle of September we were running short of fresh meat for the dogs. Nearly five months had passed since we had killed a seal, and penguins had seldom been seen. But on the 23rd we got an emperor penguin, and on the following day we secured a crab-eater seal. The return of seal-life was most opportune, as we wished to feed the dogs on meat, and seals also meant a supply of blubber to supplement our small remaining stock of coal.

During the last days of September the roar of the pressure grew louder, and I could see that the area of disturbance was rapidly approaching the ship. Stupendous forces were at work, and the fields of firm ice around the *Endurance* were steadily diminishing.

September 30th was a bad day, for at 3 PM cracks, which had opened during the night alongside the ship, began to work in a lateral direction. The ship sustained terrific pressure. The decks shuddered and jumped, beams arched, and stanchions buckled and shook. I ordered all hands to stand by in readiness for any emergency. But the ship resisted valiantly, and just when it seemed that the limit of her strength was being reached, one huge floe which was pressing down upon us cracked across and so gave relief.

"The behavior of our ship in the ice," Worsley wrote, "has been magnificent. Since we have been beset her staunchness and endurance have been almost past belief again and again. . . . It will be sad if such a brave little craft should be finally crushed in the remorseless, slowly strangling grip of the Weddell pack, after ten months of the bravest and most gallant fight ever put up by a ship."

Indeed, the *Endurance* deserved all that could be said in praise of her. Shipwrights had never done sounder or better work. But how long could she continue the fight under such conditions? The vital question for us was whether the ice would open sufficiently to release us before the drift carried us into the dangerous area which we were approaching? With anxious hearts we faced the month of October.

On the first day of that month two bull crab-eaters climbed on to the floe close to the ship and were shot by Wild. They were both big animals in prime condition, and all anxiety as to the supply of fresh meat for the dogs was removed. Seal liver also made a welcome change in our own diet.

Two or three days later we had no doubt that the movement of the ice was increasing. Frost-smoke from opening cracks was showing in all directions during October 6th. In one place it looked like a great prairie fire, at another it resembled a train running before the wind, the smoke rising from the engine straight upward; elsewhere the smoke columns gave the effect of warships steaming in line ahead.

Conditions did not change materially during the next two or three days, but on the 10th a thaw made things uncomfortable for us, and the dogs, who hated wet, looked most unhappy. The thaw indicated that winter was over, and we began preparations to reoccupy the cabins on the main deck. I also made several preparations for working the ship as soon as she was clear.

For several days the temperature remained relatively high, and all hands—amid much noise and laughter—moved on the 12th to their summer quarters in the upper cabins. On the 13th the ship broke free of the floe on which she rested to starboard sufficiently to come upright. The rudder freed itself and, the water being very clear, we could see that it had only suffered a slight twist to port at the water-line. It moved quite freely. The propeller, however, was found to be athwartship, and I did not think it advisable to try to deal with it at that stage.

The southwesterly breeze freshened to a gale on the 14th, and the temperature fell from +31° Fahr. to −1° Fahr. The wind died down during the day and the pack opened for five or six miles to the north. Our efforts, however, to force the ship out of the lead failed, and heavy pressure developed late on Sunday, the 17th. The two floes between which the ship was lying began to close, and the *Endurance* was subjected to a series of tremendously heavy strains. In the engine-room, the weakest point, loud groans, crashes and hammering sounds were heard. For nearly an hour the ship valiantly stood the strain, and then, to my great relief, she began to rise with heavy jerks and jars. The ice was getting below us and the immediate danger was past. Our position was lat. 69° 19′ S., long. 50° 40′ W.

The next attack of the ice came during the afternoon of October 19th. The two floes began to move laterally and exerted great pressure on the ship. Suddenly the floe on the port side cracked and huge pieces of ice shot up from under the port bilge. Within a few seconds the ship heeled over until she had a list of 30 degrees to port, being held under the starboard bilge by the opposing floe. Everything movable on deck and below fell to the lee side, and for a few minutes it looked as if the ship would be thrown upon her beam ends. The midship dog kennels broke away and crashed down on to the lee kennels, and the howls and barks of the frightened dogs helped to create a perfect pandemonium. Order, however, was soon restored.

If the ship had heeled any farther it would have been necessary to release the lee boats and pull them clear, and Worsley was watching to give the alarm. Dinner in the wardroom that evening was a curious affair, for most of the diners had to sit on the deck, their feet against battens and their plates on their knees. At 8 PM the floes opened, and within a few minutes the *Endurance* was again nearly upright.

Although the ship was still securely imprisoned in the pool, it was obvious that our chance might come at any moment, and watches were set so as to be ready for working ship. At 11 AM on October 20th we gave the engines a gentle trial astern. Everything worked well after eight months of frozen inactivity, except that the bilge-pump and the discharge proved to be frozen up; with some little difficulty they were cleared.

The next two days brought low temperatures with them, and the open leads again froze over. The pack was working, and the roar of pressure ever and anon was heard. We waited for the next move of the gigantic forces arrayed against us, and on Sunday, October 24th, the beginning of the end for the *Endurance* came. The position was lat. 69° 11′ S., long. 51° 5′ W.

We now had twenty-two and a half hours of daylight, and throughout the day we watched the threatening advance of the floes. At 6:45 PM the ship sustained heavy pressure in a dangerous position. The onslaught was almost irresistible. The ship groaned and quivered as her starboard quarter was forced against the floe, twisting the stern-post and starting the heads and ends of planking. The ice had lateral as well as forward movement, and the ship was twisted and actually bent by the stresses. She began to leak dangerously at once.

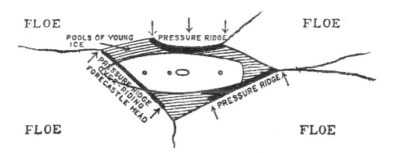

The attack of the ice is illustrated roughly in the appended diagram. The shaded portions represent the pool, covered with new ice which afforded no support to the ship, and the arrows indicate the direction of the pressure exercised by the thick floes and pressure-ridges.

I had the pumps rigged, got up steam, and started the bilge pumps by 8 PM. By that time the pressure had relaxed. The ship was making water rapidly aft, and all hands worked, watch and watch, during the night, pumping ship and helping the carpenter. By morning the leak was being kept in check.

On Monday, October 25th, the leak was kept under fairly easily, but the outlook was bad. Heavy pressure-ridges were forming in all directions, and I realized that our respite from pressure could not be prolonged. The pressure-ridges, massive and menacing, testified to the overwhelming nature of the forces at work. Huge blocks of ice, weighing many tons, were lifted into the air and tossed aside as other masses rose beneath them.

I scarcely dared to hope any longer that the *Endurance* would live, and during that anxious day I reviewed all my plans for the sledging journey which we should have to make if we had to take to the ice. As far as forethought could make us we were ready for any contingency. Stores, dogs, sledges and equipment were ready to be moved from the ship at a moment's notice.

The following day was bright and clear, and the sunshine was inspiring. But the roar of pressure continued, new ridges were rising, and as the day wore on I could see the lines of major disturbance were drawing nearer to the ship. The day passed slowly. At 7 PM very heavy pressure developed, with twisting strains which racked the ship fore and aft. The butts of planking were opened 4 or 5 inches on the starboard side, and at the same time we could see the ship bending like a bow under titanic pressure. Almost like a living creature she resisted the forces which would crush her; but it was a one-sided battle. Millions of tons of ice pressed inexorably upon the gallant little ship which had dared the challenge of the Antarctic. She was now leaking badly, and at 9 PM I gave the order to lower boats, gear, provisions and sledges to the floe, and move them to the flat ice a little way from the ship.

Then came a fateful day—Wednesday, October 27th. The position was lat. 69° 5′ S., long. 51° 30′ W. The temperature was −8.5° Fahr., a gentle southerly breeze was blowing and the sun shone in a clear sky.

"After long months of ceaseless anxiety and strain," I wrote,

. . . after times when hope beat high and times when the outlook was black indeed, the end of the *Endurance* has come. But though we have been compelled to abandon the ship, which is crushed beyond all hope of ever being righted, we are alive and well, and we have stores and equipment for the task that lies before us. The task is to reach land with all the members of the expedition. It is hard to write what I feel. To a sailor his ship is more than a floating home, and in the *Endurance* I had centered ambitions, hopes and desires. And now she is slowly giving up her sentient life at the very outset of her career. . . . The distance from the point where she became beset to the place where she now rests mortally hurt in the grip of the floes is 573 miles, but the total drift through all observed positions has been 1,186 miles, and we probably covered more than 1,500 miles.

We are now 346 miles from Paulet Island, the nearest point where there is any possibility of finding food and shelter. A small hut built there by the Swedish expedition in 1902 is filled with stores left by the Argentine relief ship. . . . The distance to the nearest barrier west of us is about 180 miles, but a party going there would still be about 360 miles from Paulet Island, and there would be no means of sustaining life on the barrier. We could not take food enough from here for the whole journey; the weight would be too great. . . .

The attack of the ice reached its climax at 4 PM. The ship was hove stern up by the pressure, and the driving floe, moving laterally across the stern, split the rudder and tore out the rudder-post and stern-post. Then, while we watched, the ice loosened and the *Endurance* sank a little. The decks were breaking upwards and the water was pouring in below. Again the pressure began, and at 5 PM I ordered all hands on to the ice.

At last the twisting, grinding floes were working their will on the ship. It was a sickening sensation to feel the decks breaking up under one's feet, the great beams bending and then snapping with a noise like heavy gunfire. The water was overmastering the pumps, and to avoid an explosion when it reached the boilers I ordered the fires to be drawn and the steam let down. The plans for abandoning the ship in case of emergency had been well made, and men and dogs made their way to an unbroken portion of the floe without a hitch.

Just before leaving I looked down the engine-room skylight as I stood on the quivering deck, and saw the engines dropping sideways as the stays and bed-plates gave way. I cannot describe the impression of relentless destruction which was forced upon me as I looked down and around. The floes, with the force of millions of tons of moving ice behind them, were simply annihilating the ship.

Essential supplies had been placed on the floe about 100 yards from the ship, but after we had begun to pitch our camp there the ice started to split and smash beneath our feet. Then I had the camp moved to a bigger floe, and boats, stores and camp equipment had to be conveyed across a working pressure-ridge. A pioneer party, with picks and shovels, had to build a snow-causeway before we could get all our possessions across. By 8 PM the camp had been pitched again.

We had two pole tents, and three hoop tents which are easily shifted and set up. I took charge of the small pole tent, No. 1, with Hudson, Hurley and James as companions; Wild had the small hoop tent, No. 2, with Wordie, McNeish and McIlroy. The eight forward hands had the large hoop tent, No. 3; Crean had charge of No. 4 hoop tent, with Hussey, Marston and Cheetham; and Worsley had the other pole tent, No. 5, with Greenstreet, Lees, Clark, Kerr, Rickenson, Macklin, and Blackborrow, the last-named being the youngest of the forward hands.

After the tents had been pitched I mustered all hands and explained the position as briefly and clearly as I could. I told them the distance to the Barrier and the distance to Paulet Island, and stated that I proposed to try to march with equipment across the ice in the direction of Paulet Island. I thanked the men for the steadiness they had shown under trying circumstances, and told them I did not doubt that we should all eventually reach safety provided that they continued to work their utmost and to trust me. Then we had supper, and all hands except the watch turned in.

But, for myself, I could not sleep, and the thoughts which came to me as I walked up and down in the darkness were not particularly cheerful. At midnight I was pacing the ice, listening to the grinding floe and the groans and crashes that told of the death agony of the *Endurance,* when I noticed suddenly a crack running across our floe right through the camp. The alarm whistle brought all hands tumbling out, and we moved everything from what was now the smaller portion of the floe to the larger portion. Nothing more could be done then, and the men turned in again; but there was little sleep.

Morning came in chill and cheerless, and all hands were stiff and weary after their first disturbed night on the floe. Just at daybreak I went over to the *Endurance* with Wild and Hurley to retrieve some tins of petrol, which could be used to boil up milk for the rest of the men. The ship presented a painful spectacle of chaos and wreck, but with some difficulty we secured two tins of petrol, and postponed the further examination of the ship until after breakfast, when I went over to the *Endurance* again and examined the wreck more fully.

Only six of the cabins had not been pierced by floes and blocks of ice. All the starboard cabins had been crushed, and the whole of the aft part of the ship had been crushed concertina fashion. The forecastle and "The Ritz" were submerged, and the wardroom was three-quarters full of ice. The motor-engine forward had been driven through the galley. In short, scenes of devastation met me on every side. The ship was being crushed remorselessly.

Under a dull, overcast sky I returned to the camp, and, having examined the situation, I thought it wise to move to a larger and apparently stronger floe about 200 yards away. This camp became known as Dump Camp, owing to the amount of stuff that was thrown away there. I decided to issue a complete new set of Burberrys and underclothing to each man, and also a supply of socks. The camp was quickly transferred to the new floe, and there I began to direct the preparations for the long journey across the floes to Paulet Island or Snow Hill.

Meanwhile Hurley had rigged his kinematograph camera, and was getting pictures of the *Endurance* in her death throes. While he was thus engaged, the foretop and top-gallant mast came down with a run and hung in wreckage on the fore-mast, with the foreyard vertical. The mainmast followed immediately, snapping off about 10 feet above the main deck. The crow's nest fell within 10 feet of where Hurley was turning the handle of his camera, but he did not stop the machine and so secured a unique, though sad, picture.

The issue of clothing was quickly accomplished, but sleeping bags were also required. We had eighteen fur bags, and so it was necessary to issue ten of the larger woollen bags in order to provide for the twenty-eight men of the party. As the fur bags were warmer, it seemed fair to distribute them by lot, but some of us older hands did not join in the lottery. Each man who received a woollen bag was also allowed a reindeer skin to lie upon.

Having apportioned the clothing we turned one of the boats on its side, and supported it with two broken oars to make a lee for the galley. The cook got the blubber-stove going, and presently I heard one man say, "Cook, I like my tea strong." Another joined in, "Cook, I like mine weak." It was good to know that their minds were untroubled, but I thought the time opportune to mention that the tea would be the same for all hands, and that we should be fortunate if two months later we had any tea at all.

During the afternoon the work continued, and the arrangement of the tents and their internal management completed. Each tent had a mess-orderly, the duty being undertaken in alphabetical order.

A quiet night followed, for, although the pressure was grinding around us, our floe was heavy enough to withstand the blows it received. "We are," I wrote on October 29th,

> . . . twenty-eight men with forty-nine dogs. All hands this morning were busy preparing gear, fitting boats on sledges, and building and strengthening the sledges to carry the boats. The main motor sledge, with a little fitting from the carpenter, carried our largest boat admirably. The ship was still afloat, with the spurs of the pack driven through her and holding her up. The forecastle-head is under water, the decks are burst up by the pressure, the wreckage lies around in dismal confusion, but over all the blue ensign still flies. . . .

The number of dog teams has been increased to seven, Greenstreet taking charge of the additional team. . . . We have ten working sledges to relay with five teams. Wild's and Hurley's teams will haul the cutter with the assistance of four men. The whaler and the other boats will follow, and the men who are hauling them will be able to help with the cutter at the rough places. We cannot hope to make rapid progress, but each mile counts. Crean this afternoon has a bad attack of snow blindness.

The weather on the morning of October 30th was overcast and misty, with occasional falls of snow. Our sledging and boating rations were still intact, for we were living on extra food brought from the abandoned ship. These provisions would provide full rations for twenty-eight men for fifty-six days, but we could count on enough seal and penguin meat at least to double this time. We could even, if progress proved too difficult and too injurious to the boats—which we had to guard as our ultimate means of salvation—camp on the nearest heavy floe, scour the neighboring pack for penguins and seals, and await the outward drift of the pack to open and navigable water. But, although this latter plan would have avoided grave dangers, I felt sure that the right thing to do was to attempt a march. It would be, I considered, so much better for the men to feel that they were progressing—even if the progress was slow—towards land and safety, than simply to sit down and wait for the tardy northwesterly drift to take us from the cruel waste of ice.

During that afternoon Wild and I went out in the mist and snow to find a road to the northeast. With difficulty we pioneered a way for at least a mile and a half and then returned by a rather better route to the camp. At 3 PM we got under way, leaving Dump Camp a mass of debris. The order was that personal gear must not exceed 2 lbs. per man, and this meant that nothing but bare necessaries could be taken on the march. I rather grudged the 2 lbs. allowance, being very anxious to keep weights at a minimum, but some personal belongings could fairly be regarded as indispensable.

Our journey might be long, and possibly we should have to spend the winter in improvised quarters on an inhospitable coast at the other end. Under such conditions a man needs something to occupy his thoughts, some tangible memento of his home and people beyond the seas. So sovereigns were thrown away and photographs kept.

I tore the fly-leaf out of the Bible which Queen Alexandra had given to the ship, with her own writing on it, and also the wonderful page of Job containing the verse:

Out of whose womb came the ice?
And the hoary frost of Heaven, who hath gendered it?
The waters are hid as with a stone,
And the face of the deep is frozen.

The other Bible, which Queen Alexandra had given for the use of the shore party, perished when the ship received her deathblow.

The pioneer sledge party, consisting of Wordie, Hussey, Hudson and myself, carrying picks and shovels, started to break a road through the pressure-ridges for the sledges carrying the boats. The boats, with their gear and the sledges beneath them, each weighed more than a ton. The sledges were the point of weakness. It seemed impossible to prevent them from smashing under their heavy loads when traveling over rough pressure-ice which stretched ahead of us probably for 300 miles.

Very heavy work followed, but both men and dogs worked splendidly. By 5 PM we had gained one mile in a north-northwesterly direction, but, although we had only gained a mile in a direct line, the deviations necessary made the distance traveled at least two miles, and the relays brought the distance marched up to six miles. Some of the dogs had covered at least ten miles. As the condition of the ice ahead was chaotic I gave the order to pitch camp.

During the night snow fell heavily, and, as the temperature had risen to + 25° Fahr., the floor-cloths of the tent were wet through. One of the things we hoped for in those days was a temperature about zero, for then the snow surface would be hard, and our gear would not be troubled by soft snow. Killer whales were blowing all night, and the ice below us was quite thin enough for them to break through if they wished, but there was no other camping ground within reach and we had to take the risk.

When morning came it was snowing so heavily that I decided not to strike camp, but the weather cleared later and we struck camp after lunch. I took Rickenson, Kerr, Wordie and Hudson as a breakdown gang to pioneer a path among the pressure-ridges. Five dog teams followed. Wild's and Hurley's were hitched on to the cutter and did splendidly. Indeed, fourteen dogs did as well or even better than eighteen men.

The ice was moving beneath and around us as we worked towards the big floe, and where this floe met the smaller ones there was a mass of pressed-up ice, still in motion, with water between the ridges. But it is wonderful what a dozen men can do with picks and shovels. In ten minutes we could cut a road through a pressure-ridge about 14 feet high, and leave a comparatively smooth path for the sledges and teams.

The Leader   Hurley

The Weddell Sea Party

Cheetham Crean McNeish James Wild Sir Ernest Shackleton Stephenson Howe Hurley
                Hussey Greenstreet Worsley Bakewell Hudson Green
                    Clark Wordie Macklin Sir Daniel Gooch Rickenson Hurley
                        Holness   Marston McIlroy

Hurley

The Dying Sun: The Endurance firmly frozen in

Hurley

The Rampart Berg

Hurley

The Long, Long Night   Hurley

The Returning Sun   Hurley

The End   Hurley

A Week Later

Hurley

CHAPTER FIVE

OCEAN CAMP

IN SPITE OF THE WET, DEEP SNOW, AND THE HALTS CAUSED BY HAVING to cut a road through the pressure-ridges, we managed to march nearly a mile, but with relays and deviations the actual distance traveled was nearer six miles. As I could see that the men were exhausted I gave orders to pitch the tents under the lee of the two boats, which afforded some protection from the wet snow.

Next day broke cold and still, with the same wet snow, and I decided to find a more solid floe and camp there until conditions were more favorable for a second attempt to escape from our icy prison. To this end we moved our tents and all our gear to a thick, heavy floe about a mile and a half from the wreck, and camped there. This we named "Ocean Camp." It was terribly difficult to shift our two boats, the surface being extraordinarily bad. At times we sank to our hips, and the snow was everywhere 2 feet deep.

This floating lump of ice, about a mile square at first, but later splitting into smaller and smaller fragments, was to be our home for nearly two months. With a view to preserving our valuable sledging rations for the inevitable boat journey, I decided that we should live almost entirely on seals and penguins. During these two months we made frequent visits to the vicinity of the ship and retrieved much valuable clothing and food.

As we were to live so largely on seals and penguins which were to provide fuel as well as food, some form of blubber-stove was a necessity.

This eventually was most ingeniously contrived from the ship's steel ash-shoot, and it served us successfully during our stay at Ocean Camp.

An attempt was next made to protect the cook against the inclemencies of the weather, and a party under Wild returned from a visit to the ship with the wheel-house practically complete. This, with the addition of some sails and tarpaulins stretched on spars, made a very comfortable storehouse and galley. Food, of course, was so important that I made a strict inventory of all that we possessed.

Early each morning the dog teams under Wild went to the wreck, and the men made every effort to rescue as much as possible from the ship. This was an extremely difficult task, but we succeeded in adding to our scanty stock between two and three tons of provisions, about half of which was farinaceous food, such as flour and peas, of which we were so short. This sounds a great deal, but at one pound per day it would only last twenty-eight men for three months. Previously to this I had reduced the food allowance to 9½ ounces per man per day.

I had the sledges packed in readiness with the special sledging rations in case of a sudden move, and I tried my hardest to give the utmost possible variety to our meals. We were short of crockery, but small pieces of venesta wood served well as plates for seal steaks; stews and liquids of all sorts were served in the aluminium sledging mugs, of which each man had one. Later on, jelly tins and biscuit-tin lids were pressed into the service.

Although I had to keep in my mind the necessity for strict economy with our small store of food, I knew how important it was to keep the men cheerful, and that the depression occasioned by our surroundings and precarious position could be somewhat alleviated by increasing the rations, at least until we grew accustomed to our new mode of life. I know from the men's diaries that my efforts in this respect were successful. "It is just," one man wrote, "like school days over again, and very jolly it is too, for the time being!" Later on, as the prospect of wintering in the pack became more apparent, the rations had considerably to be reduced. By that time, however, everybody was more accustomed to the idea and took it quite as a matter of course.

During all this time seal and penguin hunting was our daily occupation, and the supply, if not inexhaustible, was always sufficient for our needs. The seals were mostly crab-eaters, and emperor penguins were the general rule. No skuas, Antarctic petrels, nor sea leopards were seen during our two months' stay at Ocean Camp.

In addition to our daily hunt for food, our time was passed in reading the few books we had managed to save from the ship. Our greatest treasure was a portion of the *Encyclopædia Britannica*, which was continually used to settle our many arguments. The sailors on one occasion were heatedly discussing the subject of "Money and Exchange," and when they discovered that the *Encyclopædia* did not agree with their views they came to the conclusion that it must be wrong!

The two subjects of most interest to us were our rate of drift and the weather. Worsley's observations showed conclusively that the drift of our floe was almost entirely dependent upon the winds and was not much affected by the currents. Our hope, of course, was to drift northwards to the edge of the pack, and then, when the ice was loose enough, to take to the boats and row to the nearest land. We started off in fine style, drifting north about twenty-two miles in two or three days, but our average rate of progress was slow, and many and varied were the calculations as to when we should reach the pack-edge. On December 12th, 1915, one man wrote, "We are now only 250 miles from Paulet Island, but too much to the east of it. We are approaching the latitudes in which we were at this time last year, on our way down. The ship left South Georgia just a year and a week ago, and reached this latitude four or five miles to the eastward of our present position on January 3rd, 1915."

Thus, after a year's incessant battle with the ice, we had returned to almost identically the same latitude which we had left with such high hopes a year before. But under what conditions now! Our ship crushed and lost, and we drifting on a piece of ice at the mercy of the winds.

As the drift was chiefly affected by the winds, the weather was closely watched by all of us, and Hussey, the meteorologist, was called upon to make forecasts every four hours, and sometimes even more frequently. Our first few days at Ocean Camp were cold and miserable, and at night the temperature dropped to zero, with blinding snow and drift. One-hour watches were instituted, and in such weather were no sinecure.

On November 6th, a dull, overcast day developed into a howling blizzard from the southwest, and only those who were compelled left the shelter of their tent. Deep drifts formed everywhere, but, as we drifted rapidly towards the north, we preferred the screeching blizzard, with its cold, damp wind, to the weather we had previously encountered.

Some beautifully fine days, with glorious sun, followed, and we took this opportunity to dry our sleeping bags and gear as far as possible, for they had become sodden through our body heat having thawed the snow which had drifted on to them during the blizzard. Then came several days with comparatively high temperatures, and the result to the surface of our camp was disastrous. "The surface is awful! Not slushy, but elusive. You step out gingerly. All is well for a few paces, then your foot suddenly sinks a couple of feet until it comes to a hard layer."

For some days these high temperatures persisted, and at times, when the sky was clear and the sun shining, we were unbearably hot. I had already made arrangements for a quick move in case of a sudden break-up of the ice, and I took a final survey of the men to note both their mental and physical condition, for our time at Ocean Camp had not been one of unalloyed bliss.

The loss of our ship meant more to us than we could ever put into words. After we had settled at Ocean Camp she still remained, nipped by the ice, only her stern showing and her bows overridden and broken by the relentless pack. The tangled mass of ropes, rigging and spars made the scene even more desolate and depressing.

It was almost a relief when the end came. On November 21st, 1915, one of the expedition wrote in his diary:

This evening, as we were lying in our tents, we heard the Boss call out, "She's going, boys! . . ." And, sure enough, there was our poor ship a mile and a half away, struggling in her death agony. She went down bows first, her stern raised in the air. She then gave one quick dive and the ice closed over her forever. . . . Without her our destitution seemed more emphasized, our desolation more complete. The loss of the ship sent a slight wave of depression over the camp. . . . I doubt if there was one amongst us who did not feel some personal emotion when Sir

Ernest, standing on the top of the lookout, said somewhat sadly and quietly, "She's gone, boys." It must, however, be said that we did not give way to depression for long.

Indeed, these were rather miserable days, for, with the high temperature, surface-thaw set in, and our bags and clothes were soaked and sodden. To counteract depression I slightly increased our rations, and this had a splendid effect. Also, owing possibly to the prospects of an early release, our perpetual soakings did not seem greatly to trouble us. The continuance of southerly winds exceeded our best hopes, and by the middle of December I concluded that the ice around us was rotting and breaking up, and that the moment of deliverance was approaching.

After discussing the question with Wild, I, on December 20th, informed all hands that I meant to try and make a march to the west, so that we could reduce the distance between us and Paulet Island. A buzz of pleasurable anticipation went round the camp, and everyone was anxious to get on the move. So on the following day Wild, Crean, Hurley and I, with dog teams, set out westward to survey the route.

After traveling about seven miles we mounted a small berg, and the only place which, as far as we could see, appeared likely to be formidable was a very much cracked-up area between the old floe on which we were and the first of the series of young flat floes about half a mile away.

I decided to keep December 22nd as Christmas Day, and then we consumed most of our small remaining stock of luxuries. For the last time for eight months we really had as much as we could eat. Anchovies in oil, baked beans, and jugged hare made a glorious mixture, such as we had not dreamed of since our school days. Everybody was working at high pressure, packing and repacking sledges and so forth; and as I looked round at the eager faces of the men I could not but hope that this time the fates would be kinder to us than they had been in our last attempt to march across the ice to safety.

CHAPTER SIX

THE MARCH BETWEEN

AT 3 AM ON DECEMBER 23rd ALL HANDS WERE ROUSED FOR THE purpose of sledging the two boats, the *James Caird* and the *Dudley Docker,* over the dangerously cracked portion to the first of the young floes while the surface still held its night crust. Hot coffee was served, and we started off at half-past four.

Practically all hands had to be harnessed to each boat in succession, and, after much labor and care, we got both boats over the danger zone. We then returned to Ocean Camp for the tents and the rest of the sledges, and pitched camp by the boats, about one and a quarter miles off. Everybody turned in at 2 PM, for I intended to sleep by day and march by night, in order to take advantage of the slightly lower temperatures and consequent harder surfaces.

We were off again some six hours later, but were soon brought to a halt by a large open lead, whereupon we camped and turned in without a meal. I was anxious, now that we had started, that every effort should be made to extricate ourselves, and this temporary check was rather annoying. So, during that afternoon, Wild and I skied out to the crack and found that it had closed up again. We marked out the track with small flags as we returned.

Each day, after all hands had turned in, Wild and I went ahead for two miles or so to reconnoiter the next day's route, marking it with pieces of wood, tins and small flags. It was the duty of the dog-drivers to prepare the track for those who were toiling behind with the heavy boats. These boats were hauled in relays, about sixty yards at a time.

Fearing the ice might crack between them and that we should be unable to reach the boat which was in the rear, I did not wish them to be separated by too great a distance. It was grueling for the men, who worked splendidly. The dogs also were wonderful; without them we could never have transported half the food and gear which we did.

On December 25th, the third day of our march, we wished one another a "Merry Christmas," and as we sat down to our "lunch" of stale, thin bannock and a mug of thin cocoa, we also wondered what they were having at home. But all hands were very cheerful, the prospect of relief from the monotony of life on the floe raising our spirits. High temperatures during Christmas Day made the surface very trying, and at each step we went in over our knees in the soft, wet snow.

The surface was much better on the following day, but the route lay over very hummocky floes, and much work with pick and shovel was required to make it passable for the boat sledges, which were handled in relays by eighteen men under Worsley. On soft surfaces it was killing work.

Had it not been for these cumbrous boats we should have got along at a great rate, but on no account did we dare to abandon them. As it was we had left one boat, the *Stancomb Wills*, behind at Ocean Camp, and the remaining two would barely accommodate the whole party when we could leave the floe.

Still, however, we struggled on with fair success until the early morning of the 28th, when the surface was very soft and our progress, consequently, was slow and tiring. We camped at 5:30 AM, and I climbed a small tilted berg and saw that the country immediately ahead of us was much broken up. Great open leads intersected the floes at all angles, and the outlook was most unpromising.

On December 29th I wrote: "After a further reconnaissance, the ice ahead proved quite unnegotiable, so at 8:30 PM last night, to the intense disappointment of all, instead of forging ahead, we had to retire half a mile so as to get on a stronger floe, and by 10 PM we had camped and all hands turned in again. The extra sleep was much needed, however disheartening the check may be."

During the night a crack formed right across the floe, so we hurriedly shifted to a strong old floe about a mile and a half to the east of our position. The ice all around was too broken and soft to sledge over, and yet there was not enough open water to allow us to launch the boats with any degree of safety.

We had been on the march for seven days; rations were short and the men were weak. They were worn out with the hard pulling over soft surfaces, and our stock of sledging food was very small. We had marched seven and a half miles in a direct line, and at this rate it would have taken us over 300 days to reach the land away to the west. As we only had food for forty-two days there was no alternative but to camp once more on the floe and to possess our souls in patience until conditions appeared more favorable for a renewal of the attempt to escape. To this end, we stacked our surplus provisions, the reserve sledging rations being kept lashed on the sledges, and brought what gear we could from our but lately deserted Ocean Camp.

Our new home, which we were to occupy for nearly three and a half months, we called "Patience Camp."

CHAPTER SEVEN

PATIENCE CAMP

THE APATHY WHICH SEEMED TO FALL UPON SOME OF THE MEN AT OUR great disappointment was soon dispelled. Parties were sent out daily to look for seals and penguins, for our supply of food was a cause of perpetual anxiety—so small and inadequate was it. I sent Hurley and Macklin to bring back the food we had left at Ocean Camp, and they returned with quite a good load.

We were, of course, very short of the farinaceous element in our diet. The flour would last ten weeks. After that our sledging rations would last us less than three months. Our meals had to consist mainly of seal and penguin, and, although this was such a valuable antidote against scurvy that not a single case of the disease occurred among our party, it was nevertheless a badly adjusted diet, and we felt weak and enervated in consequence.

The cook deserved much praise for the way he stuck to his job under very severe conditions. At first his galley was only partially protected, and the eddies drove the pungent blubber smoke in all directions. After a few days we were able to build him an igloo of ice blocks, with a tarpaulin over the top as a roof.

"Our rations," I wrote at this time, "are just sufficient to keep us alive, but we all feel that we could eat twice as much as we get. . . . Our craving for bread and butter is very real, not because we cannot get it, but because the system feels the need of it."

Owing to this shortage of food, and the fact that we needed all we could get for ourselves, I had to order all the dogs except two teams to be shot. It was the worst job we had had throughout the expedition, and we felt their loss keenly. I continually rearranged the weekly menu, for the slightest variation was of great value, and the mere fact that the men did not know what was coming gave them a sort of mental speculation.

On January 26th I wrote: "We are now very short of blubber, and, in consequence, one stove has to be shut down. We only get one hot beverage a day, tea at breakfast. For the rest we have iced water. Sometimes we are even short of this, so we take a few chips of ice in a tobacco tin to bed with us. In the morning there is about a spoonful of water in the tin, and one has to lie very still all night so as not to spill it."

To provide some variety in the food, I began to use the sledging ration at half strength twice a week.

The ice between us and Ocean Camp was very broken, but I decided to send Macklin and Hurley back with their dogs to see if there was anymore food which could be added to our scanty stock. I gave them written instructions to take no undue risk or cross any wide-open leads, and, although they both fell more than once through the thin ice up to their waists, they managed to reach the camp. It looked, they said, "like a village that had been razed to the ground and deserted by its inhabitants." They collected what food they could find and brought it back to the camp, and as their report seemed to show that the road was favorable, on February 2nd I sent back eighteen men under Wild to bring all the remainder of the food and the third boat, the *Stancomb Wills.* This excursion was also successful, and one excellent result of the trip was the recovery of two cases of lentils weighing 42 lbs. each.

On the following day Macklin and Crean also started to the camp to make a further selection of the gear, but they found that several leads had opened up during the night, and they had to return when within a mile and a half of their destination. We were never again able to reach the abandoned camp, but there was very little left there which would have been useful to us.

By the middle of February the blubber question was a serious one. Our meat supply was very low indeed. Fortunately, however, we caught two seals and four emperor penguins, and next day we captured forty adelies.

On Leap Year Day, February 29th, we held a special celebration, more to cheer the men than for any other reason. We used the last of our cocoa, and for the future water, with an occasional drink of weak milk, was our only beverage. Three lumps of sugar were now issued daily to each man.

Later on both seals and penguins seemed studiously to avoid us, and, on taking stock of our provisions on March 21st, I found that we had only meat enough to last us for ten days, and that the blubber would not even last for that time. So we had to make our midday meal off one biscuit.

Our meals were now practically all seal meat, with the biscuit at midday; and I calculated that at this rate, allowing for a certain number of penguins and seals being caught, we could last for nearly six months. But we were all very weak, and as soon as it seemed likely that we should leave our floe and take to the boats I should have considerably to increase the ration.

One day a huge sea-leopard climbed on to the floe and attacked one of the men, and Wild, hearing the shouting, ran out and shot it. When it was cut up we found several undigested fish in its stomach. These we fried in some of its blubber, and so had our only "fresh" fish meal during the whole of our drift on the ice.

On April 2nd the last two teams of dogs had to be shot, and the carcasses were dressed for food. We ate some of the cooked dog-meat, and it was not at all bad—just like beef, but, of course, very tough. On April 5th we killed two seals, and this, with the sea-leopard of a few days before, enabled us slightly to increase our ration; and everybody at once felt much happier—such is the effect of hunger appeased. On cold days a few strips of raw blubber were served out to all hands, and it was a wonderful fortification against the cold. Our stock of forty days' sledging rations remained practically untouched, but once in the boats they were used at full strength.

When we first settled down at Patience Camp the weather was very mild, and, as a rule, during the first half of January it remained comparatively warm and calm. This meant that our drift northwards, which depended almost entirely on the wind, was checked. On January 18th, however, we had a howling southwesterly gale, which increased next day to a regular blizzard with much drift. This lasted for six days, and then the drift subsided somewhat, although the southerly wind continued, and we were able to get a glimpse of the sun. This showed us to have drifted eighty-four miles north in six days, the longest drift we had made. By this amazing leap we had crossed the Antarctic Circle, and were now 146 miles from the nearest land to the west of us—Snow Hill—and 357 miles from the South Orkneys, the first land directly to the north of us.

The wind was now the vital factor with us and the one topic of any real interest. Varying fortunes followed, but on March 13th a southeasterly gale sprang up and lasted for five days. This sent us twenty miles north, and from this date our good fortune, as far as the wind was concerned, never left us for any length of time.

On the 20th we experienced the worst blizzard we had met up to this time, though still worse were to come after we had landed on Elephant Island. As the blizzard eased up, the temperature dropped and it became bitterly cold; and in our weak condition, with torn, greasy clothes, we felt these sudden variations in temperature much more than we should otherwise have done. For two or three days it was impossible to do anything but get inside one's frozen sleeping bag and try to get warm. Too cold to read or sew, we had to keep our hands well inside and pass the time in talking to each other.

Two days of brilliant warm sunshine succeeded this period of cold, and on March 29th we experienced what was to us the most amazing weather. It began to rain hard, and we had seen no rain since leaving South Georgia sixteen months before. We regarded it as our first touch with civilization.

Although the general drift of our ice-floe had indicated that we must eventually drift north, our progress in that direction was by no means uninterrupted. We were at the mercy of the wind, and could no more control our drift than we could control the weather.

By February 22nd we were still eighty miles from Paulet Island, which was now our objective. There was a hut there and some stores which had been taken there by the ship which went to the rescue of Nordenskjöld's expedition in 1904, and whose fitting out and equipment I had been in charge of. We remarked how strange it would be if these very cases of provisions, which I had ordered and sent out so many years previously, were now to support us during the coming winter.

But this was not to be. By March 17th we were exactly on a level with Paulet Island, but sixty miles to the east. It might have been 600 miles for all the chance we had of reaching it by sledging across the broken ice in the condition in which it was at that time.

Subsequently our thoughts turned first towards the Danger Islands and then towards Joinville Island; but in each case it would have been ridiculous to attempt to reach the land, for the ice was too loose and broken to march over, and yet not open enough for us to be able to launch our boats.

For the next few days we saw ourselves slowly drifting past the land which we could not reach, and towards the end of March we saw Mount Haddington fade away into the distance.

Our hopes were now centered on Elephant Island or Clarence Island, which lay 100 miles almost due north of us. If we failed to reach either of them we could try for South Georgia, but our chances of reaching it were very small.

→ CHAPTER EIGHT ←

EFFORTS TO ESCAPE FROM THE ICE

AT DAYLIGHT ON APRIL 7th THE LONG-DESIRED PEAK OF CLARENCE Island came into view, but not until Worsley, Wild and Hurley had unanimously confirmed my observation was I satisfied that I was really looking at land. The island was still more than sixty miles away, but to our eyes it had something of the appearance of home. The longing to feel solid earth under our feet filled our hearts.

I wrote on this day:

> The swell is more marked today, and I feel sure we are at the verge of the floe-ice. One strong gale followed by a calm would scatter the pack, I think, and then we could push through. I have been thinking much of our prospects. . . . The island is the last outpost of the south and our final chance of a landing place. Beyond it lies the broad Atlantic. Our little boats may be compelled any day now to sail unsheltered over the open sea, with a thousand leagues of ocean separating them from the land to the north and east. It seems vital that we should land on Clarence Island or its neighbor, Elephant Island.

A little later, after reviewing the whole situation in the light of our circumstances, I made up my mind that we should try to reach Deception Island. Clarence Island and Elephant Island lay comparatively near to us and were separated by some eighty miles of water from

Prince George Island, which was about 150 miles away from our camp on the berg. From this island a chain of similar islands extends westward, terminating in Deception Island.

We knew from the Admiralty sailing directions that there were stores for the use of shipwrecked mariners on Deception Island, and it was possible that the summer whalers had not yet deserted its harbor. Also we knew that a small church had been erected there for the benefit of the whalers, and from this building we could get a supply of timber and construct a reasonably seaworthy boat if dire necessity compelled us. In any case, the worst that could befall us when we had reached Deception Island would be a wait until the whalers returned about the middle of November.

The swell increased on the night of April 7ᵗʰ, and the movement of the ice became more pronounced. The situation was rapidly becoming critical, and it was imperative that we should get solid ground under our feet as quickly as possible. There were twenty-eight men on our floating cake of ice, which was steadily dwindling under the influence of wind, weather, charging floes and heavy swell. I confess that the burden of responsibility sat heavily on my shoulders, but, on the other hand, I was stimulated and cheered by the loyal attitude of the men.

At 6:30 PM a particularly heavy shock went through our floe. The watchman and other members of the party made an immediate inspection, and found a crack right under the *James Caird* and between the two other boats and the main camp. Within five minutes the boats were over the crack and close to the tents. We were now on a triangular raft of ice, the three sides measuring, roughly, 90, 100, and 120 yards. I felt that the time for launching the boats was approaching; indeed, it was obvious that, even if the conditions were unfavorable for a start during the coming day, we could not stay safely on the floe much longer, for the floe might split right under our camp. If anything of the kind occurred we had made preparations for quick action, but our case would have been desperate if the ice had broken into small pieces not large enough to support our party, and not loose enough to permit us the use of the boats.

The following day was Sunday, but it was no day of rest for us. In fact it saw both our forced departure from the floe on which we had lived for nearly six months and also the start of our journeyings in the boats.

"This," I wrote, "has been an eventful day for us. . . . At 7 AM the long swell from the northwest was coming in more freely than on the previous day and was driving the floes together in the utmost confusion. . . . Our own floe was suffering in the general disturbance, and after breakfast I ordered the tents to be struck and everything prepared for an immediate start when the boats could be launched."

I had decided to take the *James Caird* myself, with Wild and eleven men. This was the largest of our boats, and she carried the major portion of our stores. Worsley bad charge of the *Dudley Docker* with nine men, and Hudson and Crean were the senior men in the *Stancomb Wills*.

Soon after breakfast the ice closed again, and we were standing by, with our preparations as complete as we could make them, when at 11 AM our floe suddenly split right across under the boats. We rushed our gear on to the larger of the two pieces, and watched anxiously for the next development. The crack had cut right through the site of my tent. Our home was being shattered under our feet, and we had a sense of loss and incompleteness hard to describe, for during all those months on the floe we had almost ceased to realize that it was but a sheet of ice floating on unfathomed seas.

The call to action came at 1 PM, after we had all eaten a good meal of seal meat. We could not take all our meat with us, so we regarded each pound eaten as a pound saved! The *Dudley Docker* and the *Stancomb Wills* were quickly launched. Stores were thrown in, and the two boats were pulled clear of the immediate floes towards a pool of open water three miles broad, in which floated a lone and mighty berg.

The *James Caird* was the last boat to leave, heavily loaded with stores and odds and ends of camp equipment. Many things regarded by us as essentials at that time were to be discarded later on. Man can sustain life with very scanty means, and the trappings of civilization are soon cast aside in the face of stern realities.

The three boats were a mile away from our floe home at 2 PM, and then we had a narrow escape from a rush of foam-clad water and tossing ice that approached us, like the tidal bore of a river. It was an unusual and startling experience; the effect of tidal action on ice is not often as marked as it was on that day, and if we had failed to pull clear of the advancing ice, accompanied as it was by a large wave, we should certainly have been swamped.

For an hour we pulled hard to windward of the berg which lay in the open water. The swell was crashing on its perpendicular sides and throwing spray to a height of 60 feet. Under other conditions we might have paused to have admired the spectacle; but night was coming on fast, and we needed a camping place. So we hastened forward in the twilight in search of a flat, old floe, and presently found a fairly large piece rocking in the swell. It was not by any means an ideal camping place, but darkness had overtaken us. We hauled the boats up, and by 8 PM the tents were pitched and the blubber-stove was burning cheerily. Soon all hands were well fed and happy in their tents, and snatches of song came to me as I wrote up my log.

An intangible feeling of uneasiness made me leave my tent about 11 PM to glance round the quiet camp, and I had started to walk across the floe to warn the watchman to look carefully for cracks when the floe lifted on the crest of a swell and cracked under my feet as I was passing the men's tent.

The men were in one of the dome-shaped tents, and it began to stretch apart as the ice opened. A muffled sound, suggestive of suffocation, came from the stretching tent. I rushed forward, helped some men to come out from under the canvas, and called out, "Are you all right?" "There are two in the water," someone answered.

The crack had widened to about 4 feet, and as I threw myself down at the edge I saw a whitish object floating in the water. It was a sleeping bag with a man inside. I was able to grasp it, and, with a heave, lifted man and bag on to the floe. A few seconds later the ice edges came together again with tremendous force. Fortunately, there had been but one man in the water, the rescued bag containing Holness, who was wet but otherwise unscathed.

Almost immediately the crack began again to open. The *James Caird* and my tent were on one side of the opening and the remaining two boats and the rest of the camp were on the other side. With help I struck my tent, and then all hands manned the painter and rushed the

James Caird across the opening crack. We held on to the rope while, one by one, the men left on our side jumped the channel or scrambled over by means of the boat.

Finally I was left alone. The night had swallowed all the others, and the rapid movement of the ice forced me to let go the painter. For a moment I felt that my piece of rocking floe was the loneliest place in the world. But Wild's quick brain had immediately grasped the situation, and the boat was already being manned and hauled to the ice edge. Two or three minutes later she reached me, and I was ferried across to the camp.

We were now on a piece of flat ice about 200 feet long and 100 feet wide. There was no more sleep for any of us during that night, but, although our position was almost as critical as possible, we were cheered by the fact that we were on the move at last, and no longer drifting helplessly at the mercy of wind and current.

The first glimmerings of dawn came at 6 AM, and two hours later the pack opened and we launched our boats. The *James Caird* was in the lead, with the *Stancomb Wills* next and the *Dudley Docker* in the rear. Our way was across the open sea, and soon after noon we swung round the north end of the pack and laid a course to the westward. Immediately our boats began to make heavy weather. They shipped sprays which froze as they fell and covered men and gear with ice.

It was soon clear that we could not proceed safely, so I put the *James Caird* round and ran for the shelter of the pack again, the other boats following. By 3 PM we were back inside the outer line of ice where the sea was not breaking, but all hands were cold and tired. A big floeberg resting peacefully caught my eye, and half an hour later we had hauled up the boats and pitched camp for the night. Every one of us needed rest after the troubles of the previous night and the unaccustomed strain of the last thirty-six hours at the oars.

Our berg appeared well able to withstand the battering of the sea, and looked too deep and massive to be seriously affected by the swell; but it was not as safe as it looked, and when daylight came we saw that the pack had closed round it, and that in the heavy swell we could not possibly launch our boats.

The highest point of the berg was about 15 feet above sea level, and during the day Worsley, Wild and I were continually climbing to this point and staring out to the horizon in search of a break in the pack. After long hours had dragged past, far away on the lift of the swell, a dark break in the tossing field of ice appeared. I do not think I had ever quite so keenly felt the anxiety which belongs to leadership.

When I looked down at the camp I could see that my companions were waiting with more than ordinary interest to learn what I thought about it all. After one particularly heavy collision somebody shouted sharply, "She has cracked in the middle." This turned out to be a mere surface-break in the snow, but the carpenter mentioned calmly that earlier in the day he had actually gone adrift on a fragment of ice. He had been standing near the edge of our camping ground when the ice under his feet parted from the parent mass, but a quick jump over the widening gap saved him.

The hours dragged on. One of the anxieties in my mind was the chance that the current would drive us through the eighty-mile gap between Clarence Island and Prince George Island into the open Atlantic; but slowly the open water came nearer, and at noon it had almost reached us. A long lane, narrow but navigable, stretched out to the southwest horizon.

Our chance came a little later, and we rushed our boats over the edge of the reeling berg and swung them clear of the ice-foot as it rose beneath them. We flung stores and gear aboard and within a few minutes were away. With the rolling ice on either side of us the three boats made progress down the lane, and presently we saw a wider stretch of water to the west which seemed to offer us release from the grip of the pack. At the head of an ice-tongue, which nearly closed the gap leading to this wider stretch, was a wave-worn berg shaped like some curious antediluvian monster, an icy Cerberus guarding the way.

At dusk we made fast to a heavy floe, but our hopes of a quiet night were quickly shattered, for we were soon compelled to cast off because pieces of loose ice began to work round the floe. Constant rain and snow squalls blotted out the stars and soaked us through, and at times it was only by shouting to each other that we could keep the boats together. Nobody, owing to the severe cold, had any sleep, and since we could only see a few yards ahead we did not dare to pull fast enough to keep ourselves warm.

All around us we could hear the killer whales blowing, their short, sharp hisses sounding like sudden escapes of steam. They were a source of great anxiety, for a boat could easily have been capsized by one of them coming up to blow; and we had an uneasy feeling that the white bottoms of the boats would look like ice from below.

Early on the morning of April 12th the weather improved and the wind dropped. At dawn I looked around at the faces of my companions in the *James Caird* and saw pinched and drawn features. Wild sat at the rudder with the same calm, confident expression which he would have worn under happier conditions. But all the men, though evidently suffering, were doing their best to be cheerful, and the prospect of a hot breakfast was inspiring.

I told all the boats that directly we could find a suitable floe the cooker would be started and that hot milk and Bovril would soon make us all feel better. Away we rowed to the westward through the open pack, and the hunger of the men could be gauged by the floes they considered suitable for our camping place. At eight o'clock a respectable floe appeared ahead and we pulled up to it. The galley was landed, and presently the welcome steam rose from the cooking food, as the blubber-stove flared and smoked. Never did a cook work under more anxious scrutiny.

Worsley, Crean and I stayed in our respective boats to keep them steady and prevent collisions with the floe, but the other men were able to stretch their limbs and run to and fro in the "kitchen," as somebody called it.

The sun was now rising gloriously, our Burberry suits were drying and the ice was melting off our beards, and the steaming food had given us new vigor. Within an hour we were off again to the west with all sails set. We had been making westward with oars and sails since April 9th and fair easterly winds had prevailed. Hopes ran high as to the noon observation for position. Optimists thought that we had gained sixty miles towards our goal, and the most cautious gave us at least thirty miles. As noon approached I saw Worsley ready to take his observation, and after he had got it we waited eagerly for him to work out the sight. The result was a grievous disappointment. Instead of making a good run to the westward we had made a big drift to the southeast. After a whispered consultation with Worsley and Wild I announced that we had not made as much progress as we had hoped for, but I did not think it wise to inform the hands that we were actually thirty miles to the east of the position which we had occupied when leaving the floe on the 9th.

The question of our course now demanded further consideration. Deception Island seemed to be beyond our reach. The wind was foul for Elephant Island, and, as the sea was clear to the southwest, I discussed with Worsley and Wild the advisability of proceeding to Hope Bay on the mainland of the Antarctic Continent, now only eighty miles distant. Elephant Island was the nearest land, but it lay outside the main body of pack, and even if the wind had been fair we should have hesitated at that time to face the high sea which was running in the open.

We laid a course roughly for Hope Bay, and again the boats moved on. I gave Worsley a line for a berg ahead and told him, if possible, to make fast before darkness set in. This was about 3 PM, and towards dusk the *Dudley Docker* came beating down towards us, and Worsley reported that he had been close to the berg and had found it unapproachable.

The news was bad, but two miles away we could see a larger piece of ice, and to it we managed, after some trouble, to secure the boats. I brought my boat bow on to the floe, while Howe, with the painter in his hand, stood ready to jump. He just managed to get a footing on the edge of the floe and make the painter fast to a hummock, but there was no possibility of getting the galley ashore, so we started the Primus lamps.

The other two boats were fastened alongside the *James Caird*, but in the rough, choppy sea they began to bump so heavily that I had to slack away the painter of the *Stancomb Wills* and put her astern. Much ice was coming round the floe and had to be poled off. Then the *Dudley Docker*, being the heavier boat, began to damage the *James Caird*, and I slacked the *Dudley Docker* away. The *James Caird* remained moored to the ice, with the other two boats in line behind her. The darkness had become complete, and we strained our eyes to see the fragments of ice which threatened us.

As the light improved the wind shifted to the southeast, and drove the boats broadside on towards the jagged floe of ice. There was no time to cast off, so we had to cut the painter of the *James Caird* and pole her off, thus losing much valuable rope.

Then we pushed away from the floe and all night long lay in the open, freezing sea. The boats were attached to one another by their painters, and most of the time the *Dudley Docker* kept the other boats up to the swell, the men who were rowing being in better case than those of us who were inactive.

The temperature was down to 4° below zero, and a film of ice formed on the surface of the sea. When we were not on watch we lay in each other's arms for warmth. Our frozen suits thawed where our bodies met, and, as the slightest movement exposed these comparatively warm spots to the biting air, we clung motionless. Occasionally, from an almost clear sky, snow showers fell silently on the sea, and lay a thin shroud of white over our bodies and our boats.

CHAPTER NINE

ESCAPE FROM THE ICE

THE DAWN OF APRIL 13th CAME CLEAR AND BRIGHT, BUT MOST OF THE men were now looking seriously worn and strained. Their lips were cracked, and the beards of even the younger men might have been those of patriarchs, for the frost and salt spray had made them white. Obviously it was imperative for us to land quickly, and I decided to run for Elephant Island. The wind had shifted fair for that rocky isle, then about 100 miles away, and the pack which separated us from Hope Bay had closed up during the night.

At 6 AM we made a distribution of stores among the three boats, in view of the possibility that they might be separated. Hot breakfast was out of the question, but I gave orders that all hands might eat as much as they pleased, this concession being partly due to the fact that we should have to jettison some of our stores when we reached the open sea, and partly to the hope that a liberal meal would compensate to some extent for the lack of warm food and shelter. Unfortunately some of the men could not take advantage of the extra food owing to sea sickness, and it was hard indeed that this devastating sickness should have been added to the sufferings which they already had to bear.

We ran before the wind through the loose pack, a man in the bow of each boat trying to pole off with a broken oar the lumps of ice which could not be avoided. I regarded speed as essential. The *James Caird* was in the lead and bore the brunt of the encounters with the lurking fragments, then came the *Dudley Docker,* and the *Stancomb*

Wills followed. I gave orders that the boats should keep thirty to forty yards apart, so that the danger of a collision, if one boat was checked by the ice, should be reduced.

We made our way through the lanes until at noon we suddenly shot out of the pack into the open ocean. Sails were soon up, and, with the sun shining brightly, we enjoyed for a few hours a sense of the freedom and magic of the sea. At last we were free from the ice, in water which our ships could navigate; thoughts of home came to birth once more, and the difficulties ahead of us dwindled in fancy almost to nothing.

During the afternoon the wind freshened and the deeply laden boats shipped much water, and steered badly in the rising sea. I had laid the course for Elephant Island, and we made such good progress that, had not the danger of the boats being separated been too great, I should have been tempted to carry on through the night. But it was imperative that the party should be kept together, and also I thought it possible that we might overrun our goal in the darkness and be unable to return.

So we made a sea anchor of oars and hove to, and though we did what we could to make things comfortable during the hours of darkness there was really little that could be done. A terrible night followed, and I doubted if all of the men would survive it. The temperature was below zero and the wind penetrated our clothes and chilled us almost unbearably.

One of our troubles was lack of water, for we had emerged so suddenly from the pack into the open sea that we had not had time to take aboard ice for melting in the cookers, and without ice we could not have hot food. The condition of most of the men was pitiable. All of us had swollen mouths and could hardly touch the food. I longed intensely for the dawn, and at last daylight came; and a magnificent sunrise heralded in what we hoped would be our last day in the boats.

By this time we were all dreadfully thirsty, and although we could get momentary relief by chewing pieces of raw seal meat and swallowing the blood, our thirst was soon redoubled owing to the saltness of the flesh. I gave orders, therefore, that meat should only be served out at stated times during the day, or when thirst seemed to threaten the reason of any particular individual.

In the full daylight Elephant Island showed cold and severe. The island was on the bearings Worsley had laid down, and I congratulated him on the accuracy of his navigation under most difficult circumstances. The *Stancomb Wills* came up and McIlroy reported that Blackborrow's feet were severely frostbitten, but, unfortunate as this was, nothing could be done. Most of the men were frostbitten to some extent, and it was interesting to notice that the "old-timers," Wild, Crean, Hurley and I, were all right. Apparently we were acclimatized to ordinary Antarctic temperature, though we discovered later that we were not immune.

Progress was slow during the day, but gradually Elephant Island came nearer. We would have given all the tea in China for a lump of ice to melt into water, but no ice was within our reach. Always, while I attended to the other boats, signaling and ordering, Wild sat at the tiller of the *James Caird*. He seemed unmoved by fatigue and unshaken by privation.

About 4 PM a stiff breeze came up ahead and impeded our progress. When darkness set in our goal was still some miles away. A heavy sea was running, and we soon lost sight of the *Stancomb Wills*, astern of the *James Caird* at the length of the painter (the *James Caird* having taken her permanently in tow), but occasionally the white gleam of broken water revealed her presence. When the darkness was complete I sat in the stern with my hand on the painter so that I might know if the other boat broke away, and I kept that position during the night.

It was a stern night. Harder and harder blew the wind, and fiercer and fiercer grew the sea. The temperature had fallen very low, and it seemed that the general discomfort of our situation could scarcely have been increased. But the land looming ahead was a beacon of safety, and I think that, in spite of our pitiable sufferings, we were all buoyed up by the hope that the coming day would see the end of our immediate troubles.

Towards midnight the wind shifted, and this change enabled us to bear up closer to the island. A little later the *Dudley Docker* ran down to the *James Caird*, and Worsley shouted a suggestion that he should go ahead and search for a landing place. I told him he could try, but that he must not lose sight of the *James Caird*. Just as he left a heavy snow squall came down, and in the darkness the boats parted.

This separation made me anxious during the remaining hours of the night, for I could not be sure that all was well with the missing boat; but my anxiety was, as a matter of fact, groundless. I will quote extracts of Worsley's own account of what happened to the *Dudley Docker*.

About midnight we lost sight of the *James Caird* with the *Stancomb Wills* in tow, but not long after saw the light of the *James Caird's* compass-lamp, which Sir Ernest was flashing on their sail to guide us. We answered by lighting our candle under the tent and letting the light shine through. With this candle our poor fellows lit their pipes, their only solace, as our raging thirst prevented us from eating anything. By this time we had got into a bad tide-rip, which, combined with the heavy, lumpy sea, made it almost impossible to keep the *Dudley Docker* from swamping. As it was we shipped several bad seas over the stern as well as abeam and over the bows.

Lees, who owned himself to be a rotten oarsman, made good here by strenuous bailing, in which he was well seconded by Cheetham. Greenstreet, a splendid fellow, relieved me at the tiller and helped generally. He and Macklin were my chief supports as stroke-oars throughout. McLeod and Cheetham were two good sailors and oars. We had now had 108 hours of toil, tumbling, freezing and soaking, with little or no sleep. I think Sir Ernest, Wild, Greenstreet and I could say that we had no sleep at all.

The temperature was 20° below freezing-point. Greenstreet's right foot got badly frostbitten, but Lees restored it by holding it in his sweater against his stomach. We were close to the land as the morning approached, but could see nothing of it through the snow and spindrift. My eyes began to fail me. I could not see or judge distance properly, and found myself falling asleep momentarily at the tiller. At 3 AM Greenstreet relieved me there. I was so cramped from long hours in the constrained position I was forced to assume at the tiller that the other men had to pull me amidships and straighten me out like a jack-knife, first rubbing my thighs, groin and stomach.

At daylight we found ourselves close alongside the land, but the weather was so thick we could not see where to make for a landing. I had again taken the tiller after an hour's rest and I ran the *Dudley Docker* off before the gale, following the coast around to the north. At first this course was fairly risky, but by 8 AM we had obtained a slight lee from the land. Then I was able to keep her very close in, along a glacier front, with the object of picking up lumps of freshwater ice as we sailed through them. Our thirst was intense. We soon had some ice aboard, and for the next hour and a half we sucked and chewed fragments with greedy relish.

All this time we had seen no possible landing place, but at 9:30 AM we spied a narrow, rocky beach at the base of some very high crags and cliffs, and made for it. To our joy we sighted the *James Caird* and the *Stancomb Wills* sailing into the same haven just ahead of us. So delighted were we that we gave three cheers.

Our experiences on the *James Caird* had been similar, although we had been unable to keep up to windward as well as the *Dudley Docker* had done. The weather was very thick in the morning, indeed at 7 AM we were right under the cliffs before we saw them. We also picked up pieces of ice and sucked them eagerly. At 9 AM at the northwest end of the island we saw a narrow beach at the foot of the cliffs; outside lay a fringe of rocks heavily beaten by the surf, but with a narrow channel showing as a break in the foaming water. Unattractive as the spot was for a landing place I decided that we must risk it. Two days and nights without drink or hot food had played havoc with most of the men, and we could not assume that any safer haven was within reach.

The *Stancomb Wills* was the lighter and handier boat, and I called her alongside with the intention of taking her through the gap first to ascertain the possibilities of a landing. Just as I was climbing into the *Stancomb Wills* I saw the *Dudley Docker,* and the sight took a great load off my mind.

Rowing carefully we brought the *Stancomb Wills* towards the opening in the reef, then, with a few strong strokes, we shot through on the top of a swell and ran the boat on to a stony beach. The next swell lifted her a little farther. It was the first landing ever made on Elephant Island, and I thought the honor should belong to Blackborrow, the youngest member of the expedition, but I had forgotten that his frostbitten feet would prevent him from appreciating the honor thrust upon him.

We landed the cook with his blubber-stove, a supply of fuel, and some packets of dried milk, and also several of the men. Then the rest of us pulled out again to pilot the other boats through the channel, and within a few minutes the three boats were aground.

When I landed for the second time a curious spectacle met my eyes. Some of the men were reeling about the beach as if they were intoxicated. They were laughing uproariously, picking up stones and letting handfuls of pebbles trickle between their fingers, like misers gloating over hoarded gold. I remember that Wild came ashore as I was looking at the men, and stood beside me as easy and unconcerned as if he had stepped out of his car for a stroll in the park.

The stores were soon ashore, but our strength was nearly exhausted, and it was heavy work carrying our goods over the rough pebbles and rocks to the foot of the cliff. We did not, however, dare to leave anything within reach of the tide. There was no rest for the cook during that day. The blubber-stove flared and spluttered fiercely as he cooked meal after meal. We drank water and ate seal meat until every man had reached his limit.

The tents were pitched with oars for supports, and by 3 PM our camp was in order, and most of the men turned in early for a safe and glorious sleep.

Before getting into the tents, Wild, Worsley and Hurley accompanied me on an inspection of our beach, and we found the outlook to be anything but cheering. Obvious signs showed that at spring tides our little beach would be covered by the water right up to the foot of the cliffs. Clearly we should have to find some better resting place, but I decided not to share this unwelcome news with the men until they had enjoyed the full sweetness of comparatively untroubled rest.

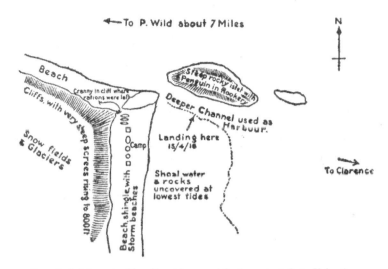

To P. Wild about 7 Miles →

N

Beach

Cliffs, with very steep screes rising to 800ft

Cranny in cliff where rations were left

Snow fields & Glaciers

Beach, shingle with storm beaches

Camp

Steep rocky islet Penguin in Rookery

Deeper Channel used as Harbour.

Landing here 15/4/16

Shoal water & rocks uncovered at lowest tides

To Clarence →

Rough sketch map of landing place and first camp at Cape Valentine, Elephant Island

The accompanying plan will show our exact position more clearly than I can describe it. The cliffs at the back of the beach were inaccessible except at two points where there were steep snow slopes.

We were not worried about food, for, apart from our rations, there were seals on the beach, and there was also a ringed penguin rookery within reach.

These attractions, however, were overridden by the fact that the beach was open to the attack of wind and sea from the northeast and east. Before turning in that night I studied the whole position most carefully, and came to the reluctant conclusion that we must move on.

Early next morning all hands were astir. The sun shone brightly and we spread out our wet gear to dry and made the beach look like a particularly disreputable gipsy camp. I had decided to send Wild along the coast in the *Stancomb Wills* to look for a new camping ground, on which I hoped the party would be able to live for weeks or even months in safety.

Wild, accompanied by Marston, Crean, Vincent and McCarthy, pushed off in the *Stancomb Wills* at 11 AM and proceeded westward along the coast. Then Hurley and I walked along the beach towards the west, searching for a place where we could get the boats ashore and make a permanent camp in the event of Wild's search proving fruitless. But after three hours' vain toil we had to turn back.

The *Stancomb Wills* had not returned by nightfall, but at 8 PM we heard a hail in the distance and soon, like a pale ghost out of the darkness, the boat appeared. I was awaiting Wild's report most anxiously, and was greatly relieved when he told me that he had discovered a sandy spot, seven miles to the west, about 200 yards long, running out at right angles to the coast and terminating at the seaward end in a mass of rock.

Wild said that this place was the only possible camping ground he had seen, and that, although in very heavy gales it might be spray-blown, he did not think that the seas would actually break over it. The boats could be run on a shelving beach, and, in any case, it would be a great improvement on our very narrow beach.

After hearing this good news I was eager to get away before the weather, which had been fine for two days, changed, and I told all hands that we should make an early start on the following morning.

The morning of April 17th came fine and clear; the sea was smooth, but in the offing we could see a line of pack which seemed to be approaching. The appearance of ice emphasized the importance of getting away promptly, for it would have been a serious matter had we been imprisoned on the beach by the pack. The preparations for leaving the beach took longer than I had expected, and, indeed, some of the men were reluctant to leave the barren safety of the beach and to venture once more on the ocean. A mishap befell us when we were launching the boats, for we were using oars as rollers, and three of these were broken, leaving us short for the journey which had still to be undertaken.

But the move was absolutely necessary, and by 11 AM we were away, the *James Caird* leading. Almost immediately a southerly gale sprang up, and we were straining at the oars with the gale on our bows. Never had we found a severer task. The wind shifted from south to southwest, and the shortage of oars became a serious matter. After two hours of strenuous labor we were almost exhausted, but then we were fortunate enough to find some shelter behind a point of rock; and there we rested while we ate our cold ration.

After half an hour's pause I gave the order to start again. The *Dudley Docker* was pulling with three oars, and she fell away to leeward in a particularly heavy squall. I anxiously watched her battling up against wind and sea, but could do nothing to help her, as the *James Caird*, being the heavier boat, was hard pressed to make any progress. The only thing to do was to go ahead and hope for the best. All hands were wet to the skin and many of them were feeling the cold severely.

We forged on slowly, and passed inside a great pillar of rock standing out to sea and towering to a height of about 2,400 feet. A line of reef stretched between the shore and this pillar, and at first I thought that we should have to face the raging sea outside, but a break in the white surf revealed a gap in the reef and we labored through. The *Stancomb Wills* followed safely, but I had lost sight of the *Dudley Docker*, and as she had been making so much leeway it was obvious she would have to go outside the pillar. It was a bad time, but I dared not pause to see what had happened to her. At last, about 5 PM, the *James Caird* and the *Stancomb Wills* reached calmer water, and we saw Wild's beach just ahead of us. I looked back for the *Dudley Docker*, but looked in vain.

Rocks studded the shallow water round the spit, and the sea surged amongst them. I ordered the *Stancomb Wills* to run on to the beach at the place which looked smoothest, and in a few moments the boat was ashore, the men jumping out and holding her against the receding wave. When I saw that she was safe I ran the *James Caird* in. We slipped the painter round a rock, and then began to get out the stores and gear, working like men possessed, for the boats could not be pulled up until they had been emptied.

We were still laboring at the boats when I saw Rickenson turn white and stagger in the surf. His heart had been temporarily unequal to the strain placed upon it, and he needed prompt medical attention. He was one of those eager souls who do more than their share of work, and who will try to do more than they are physically capable of doing. Like many of the members of the expedition he was suffering from bad saltwater boils.

I was very anxious about the *Dudley Docker*, but within half an hour the missing boat appeared and presently reached the smoother water of the bay. We watched her coming in with that sense of relief which the mariner feels when he crosses the harbor bar.

The tide was going out rapidly, and Worsley lightened the *Dudley Docker* by placing some cases on an outer rock, from which they were afterwards retrieved. Then he beached his boat, and with many hands at work we soon had our three craft above high water mark.

The spit was by no means an ideal camping ground; it was rough, bleak, and inhospitable, but some of the larger rocks sheltered us a little from the wind, and, as we clustered round the blubber-stove, we were quite a cheerful company. After all, another stage of the homeward journey was finished, and for an hour we could afford to forget the problems of the future.

The snow had made it impossible for us to find the tide-line, and we were uncertain how far the sea would encroach upon our beach. I pitched my tent on the seaward side of the camp so that I might have early warning of danger, and, sure enough, about 2 AM a little wave forced its way under the tent-cloth. After this practical demonstration that we had not gone far enough away from the sea, we took down our tents and re-pitched them close against the high rocks at the seaward end of the spit, where large boulders made an uncomfortable resting place. Snow was falling heavily, and it was difficult to see where we could find safety. Then all hands helped to pull the boats farther up the beach, and at this task we suffered a serious misfortune.

Two of our bags of clothing had been placed under the bilge of the *James Caird,* and, before we realized the danger, a wave had lifted the boat and carried the two bags into the surf. We had no chance to recover them. But this was not our only misfortune, for in the early morning our big eight-man tent was blown to pieces.

A southerly gale was blowing on the morning of April 18th, and drifting snow covered everything. The outlook indeed was cheerless, but much work had got to be done. Some sea-elephants were lying about the beach, and we killed several of the younger ones for their meat and blubber. The big tent could not be replaced, and in order to provide shelter for the men we turned the *Dudley Docker* upside down and wedged up the weather side with boulders. We also lashed the painter and stern rope round the heaviest rocks which we could find, so as to guard against the danger of the boat being moved by the wind.

The gale continued all day, while I made a careful examination of the spit to ascertain its possibilities as a camping ground. Apparently some of the beach lay above high water mark, and the rocks which stood above the shingle gave a measure of shelter. At the seaward end of the spit were the high rocks which I have mentioned, and there— we had noted with satisfaction on landing—were a few thousand ringed penguins and some gentoos.

But at 8 AM on this morning I noticed the ringed penguins mustering in orderly fashion close to the water edge. At first I thought that they were preparing for the daily fishing excursion, but presently realized that they were on the point of migrating. Hurriedly I organized a raid upon them, but we were too late; only a few of the weaker ones fell victims to our needs, the main army took to the sea and we saw them no more.

The gentoo penguins, however, remained with us, and, although they were few in numbers, the weight of their legs and breast is greater than that of the adelie, a point that particularly appealed to us.

The deserted rookery was sure at all times to be above high water mark, and we mounted the rocky ledge to search for a place on which to pitch our tents. The disadvantages of a camp on the rookery were obvious—the smell, to put it mildly, was strong; but our choice of sites was small, and during that afternoon we dug out a site for two tents in the debris of the rookery and leveled it off with snow and rocks.

My tent, No. 1, was pitched close under the cliff, and there I lived during my stay on Elephant Island. Crean's tent was close by, and the other three tents, which had fairly clean snow under them, were some yards away. The fifth tent was a ramshackle affair. The material of the torn eight-man tent had been drawn over a rough framework of oars, and thus shelter of a kind was provided for the men who occupied it.

On April 18th we took to our sleeping bags early, but my companions and I in No. 1 tent were not destined to spend a pleasant night. The heat of our bodies soon melted the snow and refuse beneath us, and the floor of the tent became an evil-smelling yellow mud. Additionally, the snow drifting from the cliff above us weighted the sides of the tent, and during the night a particularly stormy gust brought our little home down on top of us. There, however, we stayed until the morning, for it was hopeless to set about re-pitching the tent amid a raging storm and in the darkness of the night.

On the morning of April 19th the weather was still bad, and some of the men were showing signs of demoralization and were disinclined to leave their tents when the hour came for turning out. It was apparent that they were thinking more of the discomforts of the moment than of the good fortune which had brought us to sound ground and comparative safety; and only by rather drastic methods were they induced to turn to.

The southerly gale was still so severe that I was blown down as I went along the beach to kill a seal. The cooking pots from No. 2 tent at the same moment took a flying run into the sea, but as nearly all our cooking was done over the blubber-stove these pots were fortunately not essential. The galley was set up by the rocks close to my tent, in a hole we had dug through the debris of the penguin rookery. Cases of stores gave some shelter from the wind, and a spread sail kept some of the snow off the cook while he was working. He had not much idle time; the amount of seal and sea-elephant steak and blubber consumed by our hungry party was almost incredible, and he earned everybody's gratitude by his unflagging energy in preparing meals which, to us at least, were savory and satisfying.

Frankly, we needed all the comfort which hot food could give us. The icy fingers of the gale pushed relentlessly through our worn garments and tattered tents. The snow swathed us and our gear, and set traps for our stumbling feet. The rising sea beat against the rocks and shingle, and tossed fragments of floe-ice within a few feet of our boats. The consoling feature of the situation was that our camp was safe. We could endure the discomforts, and I felt that all of us would be benefited by this opportunity to rest and recuperate.

→ CHAPTER TEN ←

PREPARATIONS FOR THE BOAT JOURNEY

THE INCREASING SEA MADE IT NECESSARY FOR US TO DRAG OUR BOATS farther up the beach, and when this was done I discussed with Wild and Worsley the chances of reaching South Georgia before the winter locked the sea against us. For every conceivable reason some effort to secure relief had got to be made. The health and mental condition of several men were causing me serious anxiety, and the food supply was also a vital consideration. I did not dare confidently to count upon supplies of meat and blubber, for animals seemed to have deserted the beach, and the winter was near.

The conclusion was forced upon me that a boat journey in search of relief was necessary and must not be delayed. The nearest port where assistance could certainly be secured was Port Stanley, in the Falkland Islands, 540 miles away; but we could scarcely hope to beat up against the prevailing northwesterly wind in a frail and weakened boat with a small sail area.

It was not difficult to decide that South Georgia, which was over 800 miles away but lay in the area of west winds, must be our objective. I could count upon finding whalers at any of the whaling stations on the east coast, and, provided that the sea was clear of ice and that the boat survived the great seas, a boat party might make the voyage and be back with relief within a month.

The hazards of a boat journey across 800 miles of stormy sub-Antarctic ocean were obvious, but I calculated that at the worst this venture would add nothing to the risks of the men left on the island.

The boat would not require to take more than one month's provisions for six men, for if we did not make South Georgia in that time we were sure to go under. A consideration which also influenced me was that there was no chance at all of any search being made for us on Elephant Island.

The perils of the proposed journey were extreme, and the risk was justified solely by our urgent need of assistance. The ocean south of Cape Horn in the middle of May is known to be the most tempestuous area of water in the world, and the gales are almost unceasing. We had to face these conditions in a small and weather-beaten boat, already strained by the work of the previous months. Worsley and Wild realized that the attempt must be made, and asked to be allowed to accompany me on the voyage.

I had at once to tell Wild that he must stay behind, for I relied upon him to hold the party together while I was away, and, should our attempt to bring help end in failure, to make the best of his way to Deception Island in the spring. I determined to take Worsley with me as I had a very high opinion of his accuracy and quickness as a navigator—an opinion that was only enhanced during our journey.

Four other men were required, and, although I thought of leaving Crean as a right-hand man for Wild, he begged so hard to come that, after consulting Wild, I promised to take him. Then I called the men together, explained my plan, and asked for volunteers. Many came forward at once, and I finally selected McNeish, McCarthy and Vincent, in addition to Worsley and Crean. McIlroy and Macklin were both anxious to go but realized that their duty lay on the island with the sick men. The crew seemed a strong one, and as I looked at the men I felt confidence increasing.

After the decision was made, I walked through the blizzard with Worsley and Wild to examine the *James Caird*. The twenty-foot boat had never looked big, but when I viewed her in the light of our new undertaking she seemed in some mysterious way to have shrunk. She was an ordinary ship's whaler, fairly strong, but showing signs of the strain she had endured. Standing beside her, and looking at the fringe of the tumultuous sea, there was no doubt that our voyage would be a big adventure.

I called McCarthy, the carpenter, and asked him if he could do anything to make the ship more seaworthy. He asked at once if he was to go with me, and seemed quite pleased when I answered "Yes." He was over fifty years of age and not altogether fit, but he was very quick and had a good knowledge of sailing boats. He told me that he could contrive some sort of covering for the *James Caird* if he was allowed to use the lids of the cases and the four sledge-runners, which we had lashed inside the boat for use in the event of a landing on Graham Land at Wilhelmina Bay. He proposed to complete the covering with some of our canvas, and immediately began to make his plans.

Noon had passed, the gale was more severe than ever, and the tents were being so buffeted and battered by the wind that it did not appear possible for them to hold out for many more days. So we made our way to the snow slope at the shoreward end of the spit, with the intention of digging a hole in the snow large enough to shelter the whole party. But after examining the spot we saw that any hole which we could dig would in all probability be quickly filled by the drift.

On the following morning (April 20th) the gale was stronger than ever and no work could be done. A seal came up on the beach during that day, and so urgent was our need of food and blubber that I called all hands, and organized a line of beaters instead of simply walking up to the seal and hitting it on the nose. We were prepared to fall en masse upon this seal if it tried to escape. The kill was made with a pick-handle, and in a few minutes we had five days' food and six days' fuel stowed away in a place of safety above highwater mark.

During this day the cook, who had worked very well, suddenly collapsed, and to replace him I selected one of the men who had expressed a desire to lie down and die. The task of keeping the galley fire alight was both strenuous and difficult, and it took his thoughts away from the chances of immediate dissolution. In fact, I found him a little later gravely concerned over the drying of a naturally not over-clean pair of socks, which were hung up close to our evening milk.

There was a lull in the bad weather on April 21st, and the carpenter was able to collect material for the decking of the *James Caird*. He fitted the mast of the *Stancomb Wills* fore and aft inside the *James Caird* as a hog-back, and thus strengthened the keel with the object of preventing our boat from buckling in heavy seas. He had not enough wood to provide a deck, but by using the sledge runners and box lids he made a framework extending from the forecastle aft to a well. It was a patched-up affair, but it provided a base for a canvas covering.

We had a bolt of canvas frozen stiff, and this material had to be thawed out foot by foot over the blubber-stove so that it might be sewn into the form of a cover. When it had been nailed and screwed into position it certainly gave an appearance of safety to the boat, though I had an uneasy feeling that it bore a strong likeness to stage scenery. But, as events proved, the covering served its purpose well, and without it we certainly could not have lived through the voyage.

Another fierce gale blew on April 22nd, and our preparations for the voyage were again interfered with. Blackborrow's feet were giving him much pain, and McIlroy and Macklin thought that an operation would soon be necessary. At that time they thought that they had no chloroform, but they found some in the medicine chest after we had left.

We had begun to set aside stores for the boat journey, and to choose the essential equipment from the scanty stock at our disposal. Two ten-gallon casks had to be filled with water melted down from ice collected at the foot of the glacier; a slow business, as the blubber-stove had to be kept going all night and the watchman emptied the water into the casks from the pot in which the ice was melted. An attempt to dig a hole in the snow to provide a site for a camp failed, the snow drifting down unceasingly from the inland ice.

The weather was fine on April 23rd, and we hurried forward our preparations. About noon, however, a storm came on, with driving snow and heavy squalls. Occasionally the air cleared for a few minutes, and we could see a line of pack-ice, five miles out, driving across from west to east. This sight increased my desire to get away quickly, for winter was advancing, and the pack might soon close completely round the island and prevent our departure for days or even weeks. I did not think that ice would remain continuously around Elephant Island during the winter, because the strong winds and fast currents would keep it in motion.

Worsley, Wild and I climbed to the summit of the seaward rocks, and examined the ice from a better vantage point than the beach offered. The belt of pack outside appeared to be broken enough for our purposes, and I decided that, unless conditions forbade it, we would make a start on the following morning. The decision having been made, I spent the rest of the day looking over the boat, gear and stores, and discussing plans with Worsley and Wild.

Our last night on Elephant Island was cold and uncomfortable, and we turned out at dawn. After breakfast we launched the *Stancomb Wills* and loaded her with stores, gear and ballast, which were to be transferred to the *James Caird* when the heavier boat had been launched. The ballast weighed about 1,000 lb., and, in addition, we had gathered a number of round boulders, and a good deal of ice to supplement our two casks of water.

The stores taken in the *James Caird,* which would last six men for one month, were as follows:

30 boxes of matches
6½ gallons paraffin
1 tin methylated spirit
10 boxes of flamers
1 box of blue lights
2 Primus stoves with spare parts and prickers
1 Nansen aluminium cooker
6 sleeping bags
A few spare socks
A few candles and some blubber oil in an oil-bag

FOOD

3 cases sledging rations = 300 rations
2 cases nut food = 200 rations
2 cases biscuits = 600 biscuits
1 case lump sugar
30 packets of Trumilk
1 tin of Bovril cubes

1 tin of Cerebos salt
36 gallons of water
112 lb. of ice

INSTRUMENTS

Sextant	Sea anchor
Binoculars	Charts
Prismatic Compass	Aneroid

The swell was slight when we launched the *Stancomb Wills*, but half an hour later, when we were pulling down the *James Caird*, the swell suddenly increased, and made things difficult. Many of us got wet to the waist while dragging the boat out—a serious matter in that climate. When the *James Caird* was launched she nearly capsized, and Vincent and the carpenter, who were on deck, were thrown into the water—a piece of really bad luck as they would have small chance of drying their clothes after we started. Hurley, who had the eye of the professional photographer for "incidents," secured a picture of the upset, and I firmly believe he would have liked the two men to remain in the water until he could "snap" them at close quarters! But, regardless of his feelings, we hauled them out immediately.

The *James Caird* was soon clear of the breakers, and the *Stancomb Wills* came alongside, transferred her load, and went back to the shore for more. On this second journey the water-casks were towed behind the *Stancomb Wills,* and the swell, which was rapidly increasing, drove the boat on to the rocks, where one of the casks was slightly stove in. This accident proved later on to be serious, since some seawater had entered the casks and made the contents brackish.

By midday the *James Caird* was ready for the voyage. Vincent and the carpenter had secured some dry clothes by exchange with members of the shore party, and the boat's crew was standing by, waiting for the order to cast off. I went ashore in the *Stancomb Wills* and had a last word with Wild. Secure in the knowledge that he would act wisely I told him that I trusted the party to him, and then I said "goodbye" to the men. Within a few minutes I was again aboard the *James Caird,* and the crew of the *Stancomb Wills* shook hands with us and offered us the last good wishes.

Then, setting our jib, we cut the painter and moved away to the northeast. The men who were staying behind made a pathetic little group on the beach, but they waved to us and gave three hearty cheers. There was hope in their hearts, and they trusted us to bring the help which they so sorely needed

CHAPTER ELEVEN

THE BEGINNING OF THE BOAT JOURNEY

I HAD ALL SAILS SET, AND THE *JAMES CAIRD* QUICKLY DIPPED THE beach and its line of dark figures. The westerly wind took us rapidly to the line of pack, and as we entered it I stood up with my arm around the mast directing the steering. The pack thickened and we were forced to turn almost due east, running before the wind towards a gap which I had seen in the morning from the high ground. At 4 PM we found the channel, and, dropping sail, we rowed through without touching the ice, and by 5:30 PM we were clear of the pack with open water before us. Soon the swell became very heavy, and when it was time for our first evening meal we had great difficulty in keeping the Primus lamp alight and preventing the hoosh from splashing out of the pot.

Three men were needed to attend to the cooking, and all their operations had to be conducted in the confined space under the decking, where the men lay or knelt and adjusted themselves as best they could to the angles of our cases and ballast. It was uncomfortable, but we found consolation in the reflection that without the decking we could not have used the cooker at all.

The tale of the next sixteen days is one of supreme strife amid heaving waters, for the sub-Antarctic Ocean fully lived up to its evil winter reputation. I decided to run north for at least two days while the wind held, and thus get into warmer weather before turning to the east and laying a course for South Georgia.

We took two-hourly spells at the tiller. The men who were not on watch crawled into the sodden sleeping bags and tried to forget their troubles for a period. But there was no comfort in the boat, indeed the first night aboard the boat was one of acute discomfort for us all, and we were heartily glad when dawn came and we could begin to prepare a hot breakfast.

Cramped in our narrow quarters and continually wet from the spray, we suffered severely from cold throughout the journey. We fought the seas and the winds, and at the same time had a daily struggle to keep ourselves alive. At times we were in dire peril. Generally we were encouraged by the knowledge that we were progressing towards the desired land, but there were days and nights when we lay hove to, drifting across the storm-whitened seas, and watching the uprearing masses of water, flung to and fro by Nature in the pride of her strength.

Nearly always there were gales. So small was our boat and so great were the seas that often our sail flapped idly in the calm between the crests of two waves. Then we would climb the next slope, and catch the full fury of the gale where the wool-like whiteness of the breaking water surged around us. But we had our moments of laughter—rare, it is true, but hearty enough.

On the third day out the wind came up strong and worked into a gale from the northwest. We stood away to the east, but the increasing seas discovered the weaknesses of our decking. The continuous blows shifted the box lids and sledge-runners so that the canvas sagged down and accumulated water. Then icy trickles, distinct from the driving sprays, poured fore and aft into the boat. We did what we could to secure the decking, but our means were very limited, and the water continued to enter the boat at a dozen points.

Much bailing was necessary, but nothing could prevent our gear from becoming sodden. The searching runnels from the canvas were really more unpleasant than the sudden definite douches of the sprays. There were no dry places in the boat, and at last we simply covered our heads with our Burberrys and endured the all-pervading water. The bailing was work for the watch.

None of us, however, had any real rest. The perpetual motion of the boat made repose impossible; we were cold, sore and anxious. In the semi-darkness of the day we moved on hands and knees under the decking. By 6 PM the darkness was complete, and not until 7 AM could we see one another under the thwarts. We had a few scraps of candle, but we preserved them carefully so that we might have light at meal-times. There was one fairly dry spot in the boat, under the solid original decking at the bows, and there we managed to protect some of our biscuit from the salt water. But I do not think any of us got the taste of salt out of our mouths during the voyage.

The difficulty of movement in the boat would have had its humor-ous side if it had not caused so many aches and pains. In order to move along the boat we had to crawl under the thwarts, and our knees suffered considerably. When a watch turned out I had to direct each man by name when and where to move, for if all hands had crawled about at the same time the result would have been dire confusion and many bruises.

Then there was the trim of the boat to be considered. The order of the watch was four hours on and four hours off, three men to the watch. One man had the tiller ropes, the second man attended to the sail, and the third bailed for all he was worth. Sometimes, when the water in the boat had been reduced to reasonable proportions, we could use our pump, which Hurley had made from the Flinders' bar case of our ship's standard compass. Though its capacity was small this pump was quite effective.

While the new watch was shivering in the wind and spray, the men who had been relieved groped hurriedly among the soaking sleeping bags, and tried to steal some of the warmth created by the last occu-pants; but it was not always possible to find even this comfort when we went off watch. The boulders which we had taken aboard for ballast had to be shifted continually in order to trim the boat and give access to the pump, which became choked with hairs from the molting sleep-ing bags and finniskoe.

The moving of the boulders was weary and painful work. As ballast they were useful, but as weights to be moved about in cramped quar-ters they were simply appalling. They spared no portion of our poor bodies. Another of our troubles was the chafing of our legs by our wet clothes, and our pain was increased by the bite of the salt water. At the time we thought that we never slept, but in fact we dozed off uncomfortably, to be roused quickly by some new ache or by another call to effort. My own share of the general discomfort was increased by a finely developed bout of sciatica, which had begun on the floe several months earlier.

Our meals were regular in spite of the gales. Attention to this was essential, since the conditions of the voyage made ever increasing calls upon our vitality. The meals, which consisted chiefly of Bovril sledging-ration, were the bright beacons in these cold and stormy days. Finding ourselves in need of an oil lamp to eke out our supply of candles, we emptied one of our two tins of Virol in the manner which most appealed to us, and fitted it with a wick made by shredding a bit of canvas. This lamp was of great assistance to us at night. Since we had 6 ½ gallons of petroleum we were fairly well off for fuel.

A severe southwesterly gale on the fourth day out forced us to heave to. The delay was vexatious, since up to that time we had been making sixty to seventy miles a day, good going with our limited sail area. We hove to under double-reefed mainsail and our little jigger, and waited for the gale to blow itself out. The weather, however, did not improve, and on the fifth day we were obliged to take in the double-reefed mainsail and hoist our small jib instead.

We put out a sea anchor to keep the boat's head up to the sea. This anchor consisted of a triangular canvas bag fastened to the end of the painter and allowed to stream out from the bows. The boat was high enough to catch the wind, and, as she drifted to leeward, the drag of the anchor kept her head to windward. Thus our boat took most of the seas more or less end on, but even then we shipped a great deal of water, which necessitated unceasing bailing and pumping. A thousand times it seemed as if the *James Caird* must be engulfed; but the boat lived.

The gale had its birthplace above the Antarctic Continent, and its freezing breath lowered the temperature far towards zero. The spray froze upon the boat and gave bows, sides and decking a heavy coat of mail. This ice reduced the buoyancy of the boat, and to that extent was an added peril; but from one point of view it possessed a notable advantage. The water ceased to drop and trickle from the canvas, and the spray came in solely at the well in the after part of the boat. We could not allow the load of ice to increase beyond a certain point, and in turn we crawled about the decking forward, chipping and picking at it with what tools we had.

When daylight came on the sixth day we saw and felt that the *James Caird* had lost her resiliency. She was not rising to the oncoming seas. The weight of the ice was having its effect, and she was becoming more like a log than a boat. The situation called for immediate action. First of all we broke away the spare oars, which were encased in ice and frozen to the sides of the boat, and threw them overboard. We kept two oars for use when we got inshore. Then two of the fur sleeping bags went over the side, weighing probably 40 lb. each. We still had four bags, three in use and one in reserve should a member of the party permanently break down. The reduction of weight relieved the boat to some extent, and vigorous chipping and scraping, by which we got rid of a lot of ice, helped more. The *James Caird* lifted to the endless waves as though she lived again.

About 11 AM the boat suddenly fell off into the trough of the sea. The painter had parted and the sea anchor had gone. This was serious. The boat went away to leeward, and we had no chance to recover the anchor and our valuable rope, which had been our only means of keeping the boat's head up to the sea without the risk of hoisting sail in a gale. Now we had to set the sail and trust to its holding. While the *James Caird* rolled in the trough, we beat the frozen canvas until the bulk of the ice had cracked off it, and then we hoisted it. The frozen gear worked protestingly, but after a struggle our little craft came up to the wind again, and we breathed more freely.

Skin frostbites were troubling us, and we had developed large blisters on our fingers and hands, but we held the boat up to the gale during the day, enduring as best we could discomforts amounting to pain. Our thoughts did not embrace much more than the necessities of the hour. Every surge of the sea was an enemy to be watched and circumvented. Night fell early, and in the lagging hours of darkness we were cheered by an improvement in the weather. The wind dropped, the snow squalls became less frequent, and the sea moderated.

When the morning of the seventh day dawned there was not much wind, and we shook the reef out of the sail and laid our course once more for South Georgia. The sun came out bright and clear, and presently Worsley got a snap for longitude. We hoped that the sky would remain clear until noon so that we could get the latitude, for we had been six days out without an observation, and our dead reckoning naturally was uncertain.

The boat on that morning must have presented a strange appearance. All hands basked in the sunshine. We hung our sleeping bags to the mast, and our socks and other gear were spread all over the deck. Porpoises came blowing round the boat, and Cape pigeons wheeled and swooped within a few feet of us. These little black-and-white birds have an air of friendliness which is not possessed by the great circling albatross.

We reveled in the warmth of the sun during that day. Life, after all, was not so bad. Our gear was drying, and we could have a hot meal in more or less comfort. The swell was still heavy, but it was not breaking, and the boat rode easily. At noon Worsley balanced himself on the gunwale and clung with one hand to the stay of the mainmast while he got a snap of the sun. The result was more than encouraging. We had done over 380 miles and were getting on for halfway to South Georgia. It looked as if we were going to get through.

CHAPTER TWELVE

THE END OF THE BOAT JOURNEY

DURING THE AFTERNOON THE WIND FRESHENED TO A GOOD STIFF breeze, and the *James Caird* made satisfactory progress. I had not realized until the sunlight came how small our boat really was. So low in the water were we that each succeeding swell cut off our view of the skyline. At one moment the consciousness of the forces arrayed against us would be almost overwhelming, and then hope and confidence would rise again as our boat rose to a wave and tossed aside the crest in a sparkling shower. My gun and some cartridges were stowed aboard the boat as a precaution against a shortage of food, but we were not disposed to destroy our little neighbors, the Cape pigeons, even for the sake of fresh meat. We might have shot an albatross, but the wandering king of the ocean aroused in us something of the feeling that inspired, too late, the Ancient Mariner.

The eighth, ninth and tenth days of the voyage had few features worthy of special note. The wind blew hard during these days, and the strain of navigating the boat was unceasing, but we kept on advancing towards our goal and felt that we were going to succeed. We still suffered severely from the cold, for our vitality was declining owing to shortage of food, exposure, and the necessity of maintaining our cramped positions day and night. I found that it was now absolutely necessary to prepare hot milk for all hands during the night, in order to sustain life until dawn. This involved an increased drain upon our small supply of matches, and our supply already was very small indeed. One of the memories which comes to me of those days is of Crean singing at the tiller. He always sang while he was steering, but nobody ever discovered what the song was.

On the tenth night Worsley could not straighten his body after his spell at the tiller. He was thoroughly cramped, and we had to drag him beneath the decking and massage him before he could unbend himself and get into a sleeping bag.

A hard northwesterly gale came up on the eleventh day (May 5th), and in the late afternoon it shifted to the southwest. The sky was overcast and occasional snow squalls added to the discomfort produced by a tremendous cross-sea—the worst, I thought, which we had encountered. At midnight I was at the tiller, and suddenly noticed a line of clear sky between the south and southwest. I called to the other men that the sky was clearing, and then, a moment later, realized that what I had seen was not a rift in the clouds but the white crest of an enormous wave.

During twenty-six years' experience of the ocean in all its moods I had never seen a wave so gigantic. It was a mighty upheaval of the ocean, a thing quite apart from the big white-capped seas which had been our tireless enemies for many days. I shouted, "For God's sake, hold on! It's got us!" Then came a moment of suspense which seemed to last for hours. We felt our boat lifted and flung forward like a cork in breaking surf. We were in a seething chaos of tortured water; but somehow the boat lived through it, half-full of water, sagging to the dead weight and shuddering under the blow. We bailed with the energy of men fighting for life, flinging the water over the sides with every receptacle which came into our hands; and after ten minutes of uncertainty we felt the boat renew her life beneath us. She floated again, and ceased to lurch drunkenly as though dazed by the attack of the sea. Earnestly we hoped that never again should we encounter such a wave.

The conditions of the boat, uncomfortable before, were made worse by this deluge of water. All our gear was thoroughly wet again, and our cooking stove was floating about in the bottom of the boat. Not until 3 AM, when we were all chilled to the limit of endurance, did we manage to get the stove alight and to make ourselves hot drinks. The carpenter was suffering particularly, but he showed grit and spirit. Vincent, however, had collapsed, and for the past week had ceased to be an active member of the crew.

On the following day (May 6th) the weather improved, and we got a glimpse of the sun. Worsley's observation showed that we were not more than 100 miles from the northwest corner of South Georgia. Two more days, with a favorable wind, and we should sight the promised land. I hoped that there would be no delay, as our supply of water was running very low. The hot drink at night was essential, but I decided that the daily allowance of water must be cut down to half a pint per man. Our lumps of ice had gone somedays before; we were dependent upon the water which we had brought from Elephant Island, and our thirst was increased by the fact that we were at this time using the brackish water in the breaker which had been slightly stove in when the boat was being loaded. Some seawater had entered it.

Thirst took possession of us, but I dared not permit the allowance of water to be increased, because an unfavorable wind might have driven us away from the island and have lengthened our voyage by several days. Lack of water is always the most severe privation which men can be condemned to endure, and we found that the salt water in our clothing and the salt spray which lashed our faces made our thirst quickly grow to a burning pain. I had to be very firm in refusing to allow anyone to anticipate the morrow's allowance, which sometimes I was begged to do.

I had altered the course to the east so as to make sure of striking the island, which would have been impossible to regain if we had run past the northern end. The course was laid on our scrap of chart for a point some thirty miles down the coast. That day and the following day passed for us in a sort of nightmare. Our mouths were dry and our tongues were swollen. The wind was still strong and the heavy sea forced us to navigate carefully. But any thought of our peril from the waves was buried beneath the consciousness of our raging thirst. The bright moments were those when we each received our one mug of hot milk during the long, bitter watches of the night.

Things were bad for us in those days, but the end was approaching. The morning of May 8th broke thick and stormy, with squalls from the northwest. We searched the waters ahead for a sign of land, and, although we searched in vain, we were cheered by a sense that the goal was near. About 10 AM we passed a little bit of kelp, a glad signal of the proximity of land. An hour later we saw two shags sitting on a big mass of kelp, and we knew then that we must be within ten or fifteen miles of the shore. These birds are as sure an indication of the proximity of land as a lighthouse is, for they never venture far to sea.

We gazed ahead with increasing eagerness, and at 12:30 PM, through a rift in the clouds, McCarthy caught a glimpse of the black cliffs of South Georgia, just fourteen days after our departure from Elephant Island. It was a glad moment. Thirst-ridden, chilled, and weak as we were, happiness irradiated us. The job was nearly done.

We stood in towards the shore to look for a landing place, and presently we could see the green tussock-grass on the ledges above the surf-beaten rocks. Ahead of us, and to the south, blind rollers showed the presence of uncharted reefs along the coast. The rocky coast appeared to descend sheer to the sea. Our need of water and rest was almost desperate, but to have attempted a landing at that time would have been suicidal.

Night was approaching and the weather indications were unfavorable. We could do nothing but haul off until the following morning, so we stood away on the starboard tack until we had made what appeared to be a safe offing. Then we hove to in the high westerly swell. The hours passed slowly as we waited the dawn; our thirst was a torment and we could scarcely touch our food, the cold seemed to strike right through our weakened bodies.

At 5 AM the wind shifted to the northwest, and quickly increased to one of the worst hurricanes any of us had ever experienced. A great cross-sea was running and the wind simply shrieked as it converted the whole seascape into a haze of driving spray. Down into the valleys, up to tossing heights, straining until her seams opened, swung our little boat, brave still but laboring heavily. We knew that the wind and set of the sea were driving us ashore, but we could do nothing.

The dawn revealed a storm-torn ocean, and the morning passed without bringing us a sight of the land; but at 1 PM, through a rift in the flying mists, we got a glimpse of the huge crags of the island and realized that our position had become desperate. We were on a dead lee shore, and we could gauge our approach to the unseen cliffs by the roar of the breakers against the sheer walls of rock. I ordered the double-reefed mainsail to be set in the hope that we might claw off, and this attempt increased the strain upon the boat.

The *James Caird* was bumping heavily, and the water was pouring in everywhere. Our thirst was forgotten in the realization of our imminent danger, as we bailed unceasingly and from time to time adjusted our weights; occasional glimpses showed that the shore was nearer.

I knew that Annewkow Island lay to the south of us, but our small and badly marked chart showed uncertain reefs in the passage between the island and the mainland, and I dared not trust it, though, as a last resort, we could try to lie under the lee of the island.

The afternoon wore away as we edged down the coast, and the approach of evening found us still some distance from Annewkow Island; dimly in the twilight we could see a snow-capped mountain looming above us. The chance of surviving the night seemed small, and I think most of us felt that the end was very near. Just after 6 PM, as the boat was in the yeasty backwash from the seas flung from this ironbound coast, just when things looked their worst, they changed for the best; so thin is the line which divides success from failure.

The wind suddenly shifted, and we were free once more to make an offing. Almost as soon as the gale eased the pin which locked the mast to the thwart fell out. Throughout the hurricane it must have been on the point of doing this, and if it had nothing could have saved us. The mast would have snapped like a carrot. Our backstays had carried away once before, when iced up, and were not too strongly fastened. We were thankful indeed for the mercy which had held the pin in its place during the hurricane.

We stood offshore again, tired almost to the point of apathy. Our water had long been finished. The last was about a pint of hairy liquid, which we strained through a bit of gauze from the medicine chest. The pangs of thirst attacked us with redoubled intensity, and I felt that at almost any risk we must make a landing on the following day. The night wore on. We were very tired and longed for day. When at last dawn came there was hardly any wind, but a high cross-sea was running. We made slow progress towards the shore.

About 8 AM the wind backed to the northwest and threatened another blow. In the meantime we had sighted a big indentation which I thought must be King Haakon Bay, and I decided that we must land there. We set the bows of the boat towards the bay, and ran before the freshening gale. Soon we had angry reefs on either side. Great glaciers came down to the sea and offered no landing place. The sea spouted on the reefs and thundered against the shore. About noon we sighted a line of jagged reef, like blackened teeth, which seemed to bar the entrance to the bay. Inside, fairly smooth water stretched eight or nine miles to the head of the bay.

A gap in the reef appeared, and we made for it, but the fates had another rebuff for us. The wind shifted and blew from the east right out of the bay. We could see the way through the reef, but we could not approach it directly. That afternoon we bore up, tacking five times in the strong wind. The last tack enabled us to get through, and at last we were in the wide mouth of the bay.

Dusk was approaching. A small cove, with a boulder-strewn beach guarded by a reef, made a break in the cliffs on the south side of the bay, and we turned in that direction. I stood in the bows, and directed the steering as we ran through the kelp and made the passage of the reef. The entrance was so narrow that we had to take in the oars, and the swell was piling itself right over the reef into the cove. But in a minute or two we were inside, and in the gathering darkness the *James Caird* ran in on a swell and touched the beach.

I sprang ashore with the short painter, and held on when the boat went out with the backward surge. When the boat came in again three men got ashore and held the painter while I climbed some rocks with another line. A slip on the wet rocks 20 feet up nearly closed my part of the story, just when we were achieving safety. A jagged piece of rock held me and also sorely bruised me. I, however, made fast the line, and in a few minutes we were all safe on the beach, with the boat floating in the surging water just off the shore.

We heard a gurgling sound which was sweet music in our ears, and, peering round, we found a stream of fresh water almost at our feet. A moment later we were down on our knees drinking the pure, ice-cold water in long draughts which put new life into us. It was a splendid moment.

→ CHAPTER THIRTEEN ←

KING HAAKON BAY

OUR NEXT TASK WAS TO GET THE STORES AND BALLAST OUT OF THE boat so that we might secure her for the night, and having taken out the stores and gear and ballast, we tried to pull the empty boat up the beach. By this effort we discovered how weak we were, for our united strength was not enough to get the *James Caird* clear of the water. Time after time we pulled together but without avail, and I saw that we must have food and rest before we beached the boat.

We made fast a line to a heavy boulder, and set a watch to fend the boat off the rocks of the beach. Then I sent Crean round to the left side of the cove, about thirty yards away, where I had noticed a little cave as we were running in. He could not see much in the darkness, but reported that the place certainly promised some shelter. We carried the sleeping bags round and found a mere hollow in the rock-face, with a shingle floor sloping at a steep angle to the sea. There we prepared a hot meal, and when the food was finished I ordered the men to turn in. I took the first watch beside the *James Caird,* which was still afloat in the tossing water just off the beach.

Fending the boat off the rocks in the darkness was awkward work, and during the next few hours I labored to keep her clear of the beach. Occasionally I had to rush into the seething water. Then, as a wave receded, I let the boat out on the alpine rope so as to avoid a sudden jerk. The *James Caird* could only be dimly seen in the cove, where the high black cliffs made the darkness almost complete, and the strain upon one's attention was great.

After several hours had passed my desire for sleep became irresistible and I called Crean. While he was taking charge of the boat she got adrift, and we had some anxious moments; but fortunately she went across towards the cave and we secured her unharmed. I arranged for one-hour watches during the remainder of the night, and then took Crean's place among the sleeping men.

The sea went down in the early hours of the morning (May 11th), and, having braced ourselves with another meal, we again started to get the boat ashore. We waited for Byron's "great ninth wave," and when it lifted the *James Caird* in we held her, and, by dint of great exertion, worked her round broadside to the sea. Inch by inch we dragged her up until we reached the fringe of the tussock-grass and knew that the boat was above high water mark. The completion of this task removed our immediate anxieties, and we were free to examine our surroundings and plan the next move. The day was bright and clear.

King Haakon Bay is an eight-mile sound penetrating the coast of South Georgia in an easterly direction. The northern and southern side of the sound were formed by steep mountain ranges, their flanks being furrowed by mighty glaciers. It was obvious that our way inland from the cove was barred, and that we must sail to the head of the sound. Several magnificent peaks and crags gazed out across their snowy domains to the sparkling waters of the sound.

Our cove lay a little inside the southern headland of King Haakon Bay. A narrow break in the cliffs, which were about 100 feet high, formed the entrance to the cove. Our cave was a recess in the cliff on the left-hand of the beach. The rocky face of the cliff was undercut at this point, and the shingle thrown up by the waves formed a steep slope, which we reduced to about one in six by scraping the stones away from the inside. Later we strewed the rough floor with the dead, nearly dry leaves of the tussock-grass, and thus formed a slightly soft bed for our sleeping bags.

Water had trickled down the face of the cliff and formed long icicles, which hung down in front of the cave to the length of about 15 feet. These icicles provided shelter, and when we had spread our sails below them, with the assistance of the oars, we had quarters which, under the circumstances, were reasonably comfortable. The camp at

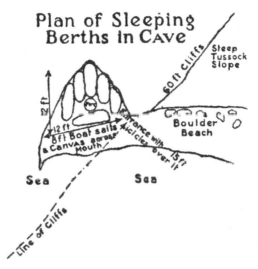

Plan of Sleeping Berths in Cave

least was dry, and we moved our gear there with confidence. We also built a fireplace and arranged our sleeping bags and blankets around it. The cave was about 8 feet deep and 12 feet wide at the entrance.

While the camp was being arranged Crean and I climbed the tussock slope behind the beach, and reached the top of a headland overlooking the sound. There we found the nests of albatrosses, and to our delight the nests contained young birds. The fledglings were fat and lusty, and we had no hesitation in deciding that some of them must die at an early age.

At this stage our most pressing anxiety was about fuel. We had rations for ten more days, and we knew now that we could get birds for food; but if we were to have hot meals fuel must be secured. Our store of petroleum was running low, and it was necessary to keep some of it for the overland journey which lay before us. A sea-elephant or a seal would have provided fuel as well as food, but we could not see a sign of either. During the morning we started a fire in the cave with wood from the top sides of the boat, and, in spite of the dense smoke, we enjoyed the warmth and the splendid stew which Crean, who was cook for the day, provided for us.

Four young albatrosses went into the pot, with a Bovril ration for thickening. The flesh was white and succulent, and the bones, not fully formed, almost melted in our mouths. That was a memorable meal. Afterwards we dried our tobacco in the embers of the fire and smoked contentedly, but an attempt to dry our soaked clothes was not successful. Until we could secure blubber or driftwood we could not afford to have a fire except for cooking.

The final stage of the journey was still before us. I realized that the condition of the party generally, and of McNeish and Vincent in particular, would prevent us putting to sea again except under pressure of absolute necessity. I also doubted if our boat in its weakened condition could weather the island. By sea we were still 150 miles away from Stromness Whaling Station.

The alternative was to attempt the crossing of the island. If we could not get over we must try to get food and fuel enough to keep us through the winter, but such a task was almost hopeless. On Elephant Island were twenty-two men whose plight was worse than ours, and who were waiting the relief which we alone could secure for them. Somehow or other we had got to push on, though several days must elapse before our strength would be sufficiently recovered for us to row or sail the last nine miles up to the head of the bay. In the meantime we could make what preparations were possible.

Shortly before midnight a gale sprang up suddenly from the northeast, with rain and sleet showers, and when daylight came the temperature was the highest we had experienced for several months. The icicles overhanging our cave were melting down in streams, and we had to move smartly when passing in and out unless one wished to be struck by the falling lumps. A fragment weighing 15 or 20 lb. crashed down while we were having breakfast.

Our party spent a quiet day, attending to clothing and gear, checking stores, eating and resting. We had previously discovered that when we were landing from the boat on May 10th we had lost the rudder. The *James Caird* had been bumping heavily astern as we scrambled ashore, and evidently the rudder had then been knocked off. A careful search of the beach and rocks failed to reveal the missing rudder, and this was a serious loss, even if the voyage to the sound could be made in good weather.

In the afternoon Crean and McCarthy brought down six young albatrosses, so we were well supplied with fresh food. The air temperature on that night was probably not lower than 38° or 40° Fahr., and the unaccustomed warmth made us quite uncomfortable in our sleeping quarters. The ice in the cove was rearing and crashing on the beach, but with firm land beneath our feet the noise of it did not trouble us.

The bay was still filled with ice on the morning of Saturday, May 13th, but the tide took it all away in the afternoon. Then a strange thing happened. The rudder, with all the broad Atlantic to sail in, came bobbing back into our cove. Nearer and nearer it came as we waited anxiously on the shore, oars in hand; and at last we were able to seize it. Surely a remarkable salvage!

The day was bright and clear; our clothes were drying and our strength was returning. In the afternoon we began to prepare the *James Caird* for the journey to the head of King Haakon Bay. During the morning of this day (May 13th) Worsley and I tramped across the hills in a northeasterly direction for the purpose of getting a view of the sound, and possibly gathering useful information for the next stage of our journey. It was exhausting work, but after covering about two and half miles in two hours we were able to look east up the bay. We, however, could not see very much of the country which we should have to cross in order to reach the whaling station on the other side of the island. Some gentoo penguins and a young sea-elephant which we found were killed by Worsley.

When we got back to the cave, tired and hungry, we found a splendid meal of stewed albatross chicken waiting for us. We had carried a quantity of blubber and the sea-elephant's liver in our blouses, and produced our treasures as a surprise for the men. Rough climbing on the way back had nearly persuaded us to throw the stuff away, but we held on and had our reward at the camp.

The long bay had been a magnificent sight, even to eyes which had dwelt long enough on grandeur and were hungry for the familiar things of everyday life. Its green-blue waters were being beaten to fury by the gale. The mountains peered through the mists, and between them huge glaciers poured down from the great ice slopes which lay behind. We counted twelve glaciers, and every few minutes we heard the great roar caused by masses of ice calving from the parent streams.

On May 14th we made our preparations for an early start on the following day, should the weather hold fair. All hands were recovering from the chafing caused by our wet clothes during the boat journey. We paid our last visit to the nests of the albatrosses. Each nest consisted of a mound over a foot high of tussock-grass, roots and a little earth. The albatross lays one egg, and very rarely two. We did not enjoy attacking these birds, but our hunger was so great that each time we killed one we felt a little less remorseful.

May 15th was a great day. We made our hoosh at 7:30 AM, and then loaded up the boat and gave her a flying launch down the steep beach into the surf. A gusty northwesterly wind was blowing, but the *James Caird* headed to the sea as if anxious to face the battle of the waves once more. As we sailed merrily up the bay the sun broke through the mists and made the tossing waters sparkle around us. We were a curious-looking party on that bright morning, but we were feeling happy.

The wind blew fresh and strong, and a small sea broke on the coast as we advanced. We had hoped to find sea-elephants on the upper beaches, and our expectations were realized. As we neared the head of the bay we heard the roar of the bulls, and soon afterwards we saw their great unwieldy forms lying on a shelving beach towards the bay-head.

We rounded a high, glacier-worn bluff on the north side, and soon after noon we ran the boat ashore on a low beach of sand and pebbles, with tussock-grass growing above high water mark. Hundreds of sea-elephants were lying about, enough to provide food and blubber for years and years. Our landing place was about a mile and a half west of the northeast corner of the bay. Just east of us was a glacier-snout ending on the beach but giving a passage towards the head of the bay, except at high water or when a very heavy surf was running.

A cold rain had begun to fall, and as quickly as possible we hauled the *James Caird* up above high water mark, and turned her over just to the east side of the bluff. The spot was separated from the mountainside by a low bank, rising 20 or 30 feet above sea level.

We soon converted the boat into a very comfortable cabin *à la* Peggotty, turfing it round with tussocks. One side of the *James Caird* rested on stones so as to afford a low entrance, and when we had finished she looked as if she had grown there. A sea-elephant provided us with fuel and meat, and that evening found a well-fed and fairly contented party in Peggotty Camp.

Our camp, as I have said, lay on the north side of King Haakon Bay near the head. The path towards the whaling stations led round the seaward end of the snouted glacier on the east side of the camp, and up a snow slope which seemed to lead to a pass in the great Allardyce range, which forms the main backbone of South Georgia. The range dipped opposite the bay into a well-defined pass from east to west.

I planned to climb to the pass, and then be guided by the configuration of the country in the selection of a route eastward to Stromness Bay, where the whaling stations were established in the minor bays, Leith, Husvik and Stromness. On Tuesday, May 16th, the weather was bad, and we stayed under the boat nearly all day. The quarters were cramped but gave full protection from the weather, and we regarded our little cabin with much satisfaction, abundant meals adding to our contentment.

A fresh breeze was blowing on the following morning, with misty squalls, sleet and rain. I took Worsley with me on a pioneer journey to the west for the purpose of examining the country to be crossed at the beginning of the overland journey. We went round the seaward end of the snouted glacier, and tramped about a mile, crossing some big ridges of scree and moraines on our way. We found good going for a sledge as far as the northeast corner of the bay, but a snow squall obscured the view and we did not get much information regarding the conditions farther on. I had satisfied myself, however, that we could reach a good snow slope leading apparently to the inland ice. Worsley reckoned from the chart that the distance from our camp to Husvik was seventeen geographical miles, but we could not expect to follow a direct line. The carpenter started to make a sledge for the overland journey, but the materials at his disposal were limited in quantity and scarcely suitable in quality.

We overhauled our gear on Thursday, May 18th, and hauled our sledge to the lower edge of the snouted glacier. The sledge proved heavy and cumbrous, and I realized that three men would be unable to manage it amid the snow-plains, glaciers and peaks of the interior. Worsley and Crean were coming with me, and, after consultation, we decided to leave the sleeping bags behind and make the journey in very light marching order.

We decided to take three days' provisions for each man in the form of sledging ration and biscuit, the Primus lamp filled with oil, the small cooker, the carpenter's adze (for use as an ice axe), and the alpine rope, which made a total length of 50 feet when knotted, and would help us to lower ourselves down steep slopes or cross crevassed glaciers.

We had two boxes of matches left, one full and the other partially used. We decided to leave the full box at the camp and to take the second box, which contained forty-eight matches. I was unfortunate as regards footgear, as I had given away my heavy boots on the floe, and only had a lighter pair in poor condition. The carpenter helped me by putting several screws into the sole of each boot with the object of providing a grip on the ice. The screws came out of the *James Caird*.

We turned in early that night, but troubled thoughts kept me from sleeping. The task before the overland party would in all probability be heavy, and we were going to leave a weak party behind us in the camp. Vincent was still in the same condition and could not march. McNeish was pretty well broken up. These two men could not manage for themselves, and I had to leave McCarthy to look after them. Should we fail to reach the whaling station McCarthy might have a difficult task.

We had very scanty knowledge of the interior, for no man had ever penetrated from the coast of South Georgia at any point, and I knew that the whalers regarded the country as inaccessible.

At 2 AM on the Friday morning we turned out, and an hour later our hoosh was ready. The full moon was shining in a practically cloudless sky, and we made a start as soon as we had eaten our meal. Our first difficulty was to get round the edge of the snouted glacier, which had points like fingers projecting into the sea. The waves were reaching the points of these fingers, and we had to rush from one recess to another when the waters receded. We soon reached the east side of the glacier, and began to ascend a snow slope, heading due east on the last lap of our long trail.

The snow surface was disappointing, and as we sank over our ankles at each step our progress was slow. After two hours' steady climbing we were 2,500 feet above sea level, and the bright moonlight showed us that the interior was tremendously broken. High peaks, impassable cliffs, steep snow slopes, and sharply descending glaciers could be seen in all directions, with stretches of snow-plain overlaying the ice sheet of the interior. The slope which we were ascending mounted to a ridge, and our course lay direct to the top. The moon, which was a good friend to us, threw a long shadow at one point and told us that the surface was broken in our path. Thus warned we avoided a huge hole capable of swallowing an army. The bay was now about three miles away.

I had hoped to get a view of the country ahead of us from the top of this slope, but as the surface became more level a thick fog drifted down. Under these conditions we roped ourselves together as a precaution against holes, crevasses and precipices, and I broke trail through the soft snow. With almost the full length of rope between myself and the last man we could steer an approximately straight course, for if I veered to the right or left when marching into the blank wall of fog, the last man on the rope could shout a direction. So, like a ship with its "port," "starboard," "steady," we tramped through the fog for the next two hours.

Then, as daylight came, the fog partially lifted, and, from a height of about 3,000 feet, we looked down on what seemed to be a huge frozen lake, with its farther shores still obscured by fog. We halted there to eat a bit of biscuit, and to discuss whether we would go down and cross the flat surface of the lake or keep on the ridge we had already reached. I decided to go down, as the lake lay on our course. After an hour's fairly easy travel through the snow we began to meet crevasses, which showed that we were on a glacier. Later on the fog lifted completely and then we saw that our lake stretched to the horizon, and suddenly we realized that we were looking down upon the open sea on the east coast of the island.

Evidently we were at the top of Possession Bay, and the island at that point could not be more than five miles across from the head of King Haakon Bay. Our rough chart was inaccurate, and there was nothing for it but to start up the glacier again. That was about seven o'clock, and in two hours we had more than recovered our lost ground.

We regained the ridge and then struck southeast, for the chart showed that two more bays indented the coast before Stromness. It was comforting to know that we should have the eastern water in sight during our journey, although we could see that there was no way around the shoreline owing to steep cliffs and glaciers.

Men lived in houses lit by electric light on the east coast. News of the outside world awaited us there, and, above all, the east coast meant for us the means of rescuing the twenty-two men left on Elephant Island.

CHAPTER FOURTEEN

Across South Georgia

THE SUN ROSE WITH EVERY APPEARANCE OF A FINE DAY; WE WERE traveling over a gently rising plateau, and at the end of an hour we found ourselves becoming uncomfortably hot. After passing an area of crevasses we paused for our first meal. We dug a hole in the snow about 3 feet deep and put the Primus into it. The hot hoosh was soon eaten, and we plodded on towards a sharp ridge between two of the peaks which lay ahead of us. By 11 AM we were almost at the crest.

The slope became precipitous, and we had to cut steps as we advanced. For this purpose the adze proved an excellent instrument. At last I stood upon the razorback, while the other men held the rope and waited for news. The outlook was disappointing. I looked down a sheer precipice to a chaos of crumpled ice 1,500 feet below. There was no way down for us. The country to the east was a great snow upland, sloping upwards for seven or eight miles to a height of over 4,000 feet. To the north it fell away steeply in glaciers into the bays, and to the south it was broken by huge outfalls from the inland ice sheet. Our path lay between the glaciers and the outfalls, but first we had to descend from the ridge on which we were standing.

Cutting steps with the adze we moved in a lateral direction round the base of a dolomite, but the same precipice confronted us. Away to the northeast there appeared to be a snow slope which might give a path to the lower country, and so we retraced our steps down the long slope which had taken us three hours to climb. In an hour we

97

were at the bottom, but we were beginning to feel the strain of unaccustomed marching.

Skirting the base of the mountain above us, we came to a gigantic gully, a mile and a half long and 1,000 feet deep. This gully was semicircular in form, and ended in a gentle incline. We passed through it, and at the far end we had another meal and short rest. This was at 12:30 PM. Refreshed by our steaming Bovril ration we started once more for the crest, and after another weary climb we reached the top. The same precipice lay below, and my eyes searched vainly for a way down. The snow, loosened by the hot sun, was now in a treacherous condition, and, looking back, we could see that a fog was rolling up behind us and meeting in the valleys another fog which was coming up from the east. This was a plain warning that we must get down to lower levels before we were enveloped.

The ridge was studded with peaks, which prevented us from getting a clear view either to the right or left, and I had to decide that our course lay back the way which we had come. It was of the utmost importance for us to get down into the next valley before dark. We were up 4,500 feet and the night temperature at that elevation would be very low. The afternoon was wearing on, and the fog was rolling up ominously from the west. We had neither tent nor sleeping bags, and our clothes were terribly weather-worn.

In the distance, down the valley below us, we could see tussock-grass close to the shore, and if we could get down we might possibly dig out a hole in one of the lower snowbanks, line it with dry grass, and make ourselves fairly comfortable for the night. Back we went, and presently reached the top of another ridge in the fading light. After a glance over the top I turned to the anxious faces of the men behind me and said, "Come on, boys." Within a minute they stood beside me on the ice ridge, the surface of which fell away at a sharp incline before us but merged into a snow slope.

We could not see the bottom, and the possibility of the slope ending in a sheer fall occurred to us, but the fog which was creeping up behind us allowed no time for hesitation. At first we descended slowly, cutting steps in the hard snow, then the surface became softer, indicating that the gradient was less severe. There could be no turning back now, so we unroped and slid in the fashion of youthful days. When we stopped on a snowbank at the foot of the slope we found that we had descended at least 900 feet in two or three minutes. We looked back and saw the grey fingers of the fog appearing on the ridge. But we had escaped.

The country to the east was an ascending snow upland dividing the glaciers of the north coast from the outfalls of the south. From the top we had seen that our course lay between two huge masses of crevasses, and we thought that the road ahead was clear. This belief and the increasing cold made us abandon the idea of camping. At 6 PM we had another meal, and then we started up the long, gentle ascent. Night was upon us, and for an hour we plodded on in almost complete darkness, watching warily for signs of crevasses. But about 8 PM the full moon rose ahead of us and made a silver pathway for our feet. Onwards and upwards through soft snow we marched, resting occasionally on hard patches. By midnight we were again at an elevation of 4,000 feet. Still we were following the light, for as the moon swung round towards the northeast our path curved in that direction. The friendly moon seemed to pilot our weary feet. We could have had no better guide.

Midnight found us approaching the edge of a great snowfield, and a gentle slope lured our all-too-willing feet in that direction. At the base of the slope we thought that Stromness Bay lay. After we had descended about 300 feet a thin wind began to attack us. We had been on the march for over twenty hours, only halting for occasional meals. After 1 AM we cut a pit in the snow, piled up loose snow around it, and again started the Primus. Worsley and Crean sang their old songs when the Primus was going merrily. Laughter was in our hearts, though not on our parched and cracked lips.

Within half an hour we were away again, still downward to the coast. We now felt almost sure that we were above Stromness Bay, and joyfully pointed out various landmarks revealed by the light of the moon, whose friendly face was by this time cloud-swept. Our high hopes were soon shattered. Crevasses warned us that we were on another glacier, and presently we looked down almost to the seaward edge of the great riven ice-mass. I knew that there was no glacier in Stromness and realized that this must be Fortuna Glacier. The disappointment was severe. Back we turned and tramped up the glacier again, working at a tangent to the southeast. We were very tired.

At 5 AM we were at the foot of the rocky spurs of the range. The wind blowing down from the heights was chilling us, and we decided to get under the lee of a rock and rest. We put our sticks and the adze on the snow, sat down on them as close to one another as possible, and put our arms round each other. I thought that in this way we might keep warm and have half-an-hour's rest. Within a minute my two companions were fast asleep, and I realized how disastrous it would be if we all slumbered together, for sleep under such conditions merges into death. So after five minutes I awoke them and gave the word for a fresh start. So stiff were we that for the first 300 yards or so we marched with our knees bent.

A jagged line of peaks with a gap like a broken tooth confronted us. This was the ridge which runs in a southerly direction from Fortuna Bay, and our course to Stromness lay across it. A very steep slope led up to the ridge and an icy wind burst through the gap. With anxious hearts as well as with weary bodies we went through the gap at 6 AM. Had the farther slope proved impassable our situation would have been almost desperate; but the worst was turning to the best for us.

The twisted, wave-like rock formations of Husvik Harbor appeared right ahead of us in the opening of dawn. Without a word we shook hands with one another. To our minds the journey was over, though really twelve miles of difficult country had still to be crossed. A gentle snow slope descended at our feet towards a valley which separated our ridge from the hills immediately behind Husvik, and as we stood gazing Worsley said solemnly, "Boss, it looks too good to be true!"

Down we went, to be checked presently by water 2,500 feet below. We could see the little wave-ripples on the black beach, penguins strutting, and dark objects like seals lolling on the sand. This was an eastern arm of Fortuna Bay, separated by the ridge from the arm we had seen below us during the night.

The slope which we were traversing seemed to end in a precipice above the beach. But our revived spirits were not to be damped by any difficulties on the last stage of our journey, and cheerfully we camped for breakfast. While breakfast was being prepared, I climbed the ridge above us to secure an extended view of the country below; and at 6:30 AM I thought I heard the sound of a steam-whistle. I dared not be certain, but I knew that the men at the whaling stations would be called from their beds about that time.

Descending again to the camp I told the others, and in intense excitement we watched the chronometer for seven o'clock, when the whalers would be summoned to work. Right to the minute the steam-whistle came clearly to us, and never had anyone of us heard sweeter music. It was the first sound created by outside human agency which had come to our ears since December 1914. That whistle told us that men were near, that ships were ready, and that very soon we should be on our way back to Elephant Island to rescue the men waiting there. It was a moment hard to describe. Pain and aches, boat journeys, marches, hunger and fatigue, were forgotten, only the perfect contentment which comes from work accomplished remained.

My examination of the country before us had not provided definite information, so I put the situation before Worsley and Crean. Our obvious course lay down a snow slope in the direction of Husvik. "Boys," I said, "this snow slope seems to end in a precipice, but perhaps there is no precipice. If we don't go down we shall have to make a detour of at least five miles before we reach level going. What shall it be?" They both replied at once, "Try the slope." So again we started downwards.

We abandoned the Primus lamp, now empty, and carried with us one ration and a biscuit each. Deep snow clogged our feet, but after descending about 500 feet we thought that we saw our way clear ahead. A steep gradient of blue ice was the next obstacle. Worsley and Crean got a firm footing in a hole excavated with the adze, and then lowered me as I cut steps until the full 50 feet of our alpine rope was out. Then I made a hole big enough for the three of us, and the other two men came down the steps. In this laborious fashion we spent two hours descending about 500 feet. Halfway down we had to strike away diagonally to the left, for we noticed that the fragments of ice loosened by the adze were taking a leap into space at the bottom of the slope. At last, and very thankfully, we got off the steep ice at a point where some rocks protruded, and then we could see that there was a perilous precipice directly below the point where we had started to cut the steps.

A slide down a slippery slope, with the adze going ahead, completed this descent, and, incidentally, still further damaged our much-tried trousers. When we arrived at the bottom we were not more than 1,500 feet above the sea. The slope was comparatively easy, and presently we came to patches of tussock-grass, and a few minutes later we reached the sandy beach. At our best speed we went along the beach to another rising ridge of tussock, and here we saw the first evidence of the proximity of man. A recently killed seal was lying there, and presently we saw several other bodies bearing the marks of bullet wounds. Later I heard that men from Stromness go round by boat to Fortuna Bay to shoot seals.

By noon we were well up the slope on the other side of the bay, and half an hour later we were on a flat plateau, with one more ridge to cross before we descended into Husvik. I was leading when I suddenly found myself up to my knees in water and quickly sinking deeper through the snow-crust. I flung myself down and called to the others to do the same, so that our weight should be distributed on the treacherous surface. We were on top of a small lake, snow covered. After lying still for a few moments we rose and walked delicately, like Agag, for 200 yards, until a rise in the surface showed us that we were clear of the lake.

At 1:30 PM we climbed round a final ridge and saw a little steamer, a whaling boat, entering the bay, 2,500 feet below. A few moments later the masts of a sailing ship lying at a wharf came in sight. Minute figures moving to and fro caught our gaze, and then we saw the sheds and factory of Stromness Whaling Station. Once more we paused and shook one another warmly by the hand.

Cautiously we started down the slope which led to warmth and comfort, but the last lap of the journey was extraordinarily difficult. Vainly we sought a safe, or reasonably safe, way down the steep ice-clad mountainside. The sole possible pathway seemed to be a channel cut by water running from the upland. Down through icy water we followed the course of this stream. We were wet to the waist, shivering, cold and tired.

Presently our ears detected an unwelcome sound which might under other conditions have been musical. It was the splashing of a waterfall, and we were at the wrong end. When we reached the top of this fall we peered over cautiously and discovered that there was a drop of 25 or 30 feet, with impassable ice-cliffs on both sides. To go up again was, in our utterly wearied condition, scarcely thinkable. The way down was through the waterfall itself.

With some difficulty we made fast one end of our rope to a boulder, and then Worsley and I lowered Crean, who was the heaviest man. He disappeared altogether in the falling water and came out gasping at the bottom. I went next, sliding down the rope, and Worsley, who was the lightest and nimblest of us, followed. At the bottom of the fall we again stood on dry land.

The rope could not be recovered. We had flung down the adze from the top of the fall, and also the logbook wrapped in one of our blouses. That was all we brought, except our wet clothes, from the Antarctic, which a year and a half before we had entered with well-found ship, full equipment and high hopes. That was all of tangible things; but in memories we were rich. We had pierced the veneer of outside things. We had seen God in His splendors, we had heard the text that Nature renders. We had reached the naked soul of man.

Shivering with cold, yet with hearts light and happy, we set off towards the whaling station, now not more than a mile and a half distant. The difficulties of the journey lay behind us. The thought that there might be women at the station made us painfully conscious of our uncivilized appearance, and we tried to straighten ourselves out a bit. Our beards were long and our hair was matted. We were unwashed, and the garments which we had worn for nearly a year without a change were tattered and stained. Three more unpleasant-looking ruffians could scarcely be imagined. Worsley produced several safety-pins from some corner of his garments, and made some temporary repairs which really emphasized his disrepair.

Down we hurried, and when quite close to the station we met two small boys ten or twelve years old. I asked them where the manager's house was, and they did not answer. They gave us one most informing look and then they ran from us as fast as their legs would carry them.

We reached the outskirts of the station and passed through the "digesting house," which was dark inside. Emerging at the other end we met an old man who gave us no time to ask any question. He hurried away. This greeting was not friendly. Then we came to the wharf, where the man in charge stuck to his station. I asked him if Mr. Sorlle (the manager) was in the house.

"Yes," he said as he stared at us.

"We would like to see him," said I.

"Who are you?" he asked.

"We have lost our ship and come over the island," I replied.

"You have come over the island?" he said, in a tone of entire disbelief.

Then he went towards the manager's house and we followed him. I learned afterwards that he said to Mr. Sorlle: "There are three funny-looking men outside, who say they have come over the island and they know you. I have left them outside." A very necessary precaution from his point of view.

Mr. Sorlle came out to the door and said, "Well?"

"Don't you know me?" I said.

"I know your voice," he replied doubtfully. "You're the mate of the *Daisy.*"

"My name is Shackleton," I said.

Immediately he put out his hand and said, "Come in. Come in."

"Tell me, when was the war over?" I asked.

"The war is not over," he answered. "Millions are being killed. Europe is mad. The world is mad."

Mr. Sorlle's hospitality had no bounds. He would scarcely let us wait to remove our freezing boots before he took us into his house, and gave us seats in a warm and comfortable room. We were not fit to sit in anyone's house until we had washed and put on clean clothes, but the kindness of the station manager was proof even against the unpleasantness of being in a room with us. He gave us coffee and cakes in the Norwegian fashion, and then showed us upstairs to the bathroom, where we shed our rags and scrubbed ourselves luxuriously.

Mr. Sorlle's kindness did not end with his personal care to us. While we were washing he gave orders for one of the whaling vessels to be prepared at once, so that it might leave that night to pick up the other three men on the other side of the island. Soon we were clean again, and then we put on delightful new clothes supplied from the station stores and got rid of our superfluous hair. Then came a splendid meal, while Mr. Sorlle told us the arrangements he had made, and we discussed plans for the rescue of the main party on Elephant Island.

I arranged that Worsley should go with the relief ship to show the exact spot where the carpenter and his two companions were camped, while I began to prepare for the relief of the party on Elephant Island. The whaling vessel that was going round to King Haakon Bay was expected back on the Monday morning, and was to call at Grytviken Harbor, the port from which we had sailed in December 1914, in order that the magistrate resident there might be informed of the fate of the *Endurance.* It was also possible that letters were awaiting us there.

Worsley went aboard the whaler at ten o'clock that night; and on the next day the relief ship entered King Haakon Bay and Worsley reached Peggotty Camp in a boat. The three men were delighted beyond measure to be relieved, but they did not recognize Worsley, who had left them a hairy, dirty ruffian and had returned spruce and shaven.

Within a few minutes the whalers had moved our bits of gear into their boat. They towed off the *James Caird,* and, having hoisted her to the deck of their ship, they started on the return voyage. They entered Stromness Bay at dusk on Monday afternoon, and the men of the whaling station mustered on the beach to receive the rescued party, and also to examine the boat which we had navigated across 800 miles of the stormy ocean they knew so well.

When I look back at those days I do not doubt that Providence guided us, not only across those snowfields, but also across the stormy white sea which separated Elephant Island from our landing place on South Georgia. I know that during that long march of thirty-six hours over the unnamed mountains and glaciers of South Georgia it often seemed to me that we were four, not three. And Worsley and Crean had the same idea. One feels "the dearth of human words, the roughness of mortal speech," in trying to describe intangible things, but a record of our journeys would be incomplete without reference to a subject very near to our hearts.

CHAPTER FIFTEEN

THE RESCUE

OUR FIRST NIGHT AT THE WHALING STATION WAS BLISSFUL. CREAN and I shared a beautiful bedroom in Mr. Sorlle's house, and we were so comfortable that we could not sleep. Outside a dense snowstorm, which started two hours after our arrival and lasted until the following day, was swirling about the mountain slopes. It would have gone hard with us had we still been on the mountains, and we were thankful indeed to be in a place of safety. Deep snow lay everywhere on the following morning.

After breakfast Mr. Sorlle took us round to Husvik in a motor launch. Avidly we listened to his account of the war. We were like men arisen from the dead to a world gone mad, and it took our minds sometime to accustom themselves to the tales of nations in arms, of deathless courage and unimagined slaughter. The reader may not realize quite how difficult it was for us to envisage nearly two years of the most stupendous war of history. I suppose our experience was unique. No other civilized men could have been as blankly ignorant of world-shaking events as we were when we reached Stromness Whaling Station.

I heard the first rumor of the *Aurora's* misadventures in the Ross Sea from Mr. Sorlle. He had heard that the *Aurora* had broken away from winter quarters in McMurdo Sound and had reached New Zealand after a long drift, and that there was no news of the shore party. His information was indefinite as regards details, and not until I reached the Falkland Islands some time later did I get a definite report about the *Aurora*. This rumor, however, made it more important than ever that the rest of the Weddell Sea party should be quickly relieved, so that I should be free for whatever effort was required on the Ross Sea side.

When we reached Husvik on that Sunday morning we were warmly greeted by the magistrate (Mr. Bernsten), who was an old friend of mine, and by the other members of the little community. Moored in the harbor was one of the largest of the whalers, the *Southern Sky*, owned by an English company, but now laid up for the winter. I had no means of communicating immediately with the owners, but, on my accepting all responsibility, Mr. Bernsten made arrangements for me to take this ship down to Elephant Island. I wrote out an agreement with Lloyd's for the insurance of the ship.

Captain Thom, an old friend of the expedition, happened to be in Husvik with his ship, the *Orwell*, loading oil for use in British munition works, and he at once volunteered to come with us in any capacity. I asked him to come as captain of the *Southern Sky*. There was no difficulty in getting a crew, for the whalers were eager to assist in the rescue of the men in distress. Indeed they started work at once, and willing hands made light labor. I purchased all the stores and equipment required, including special comforts for the men we hoped to rescue, from the station stores. And on Tuesday morning the *Southern Sky* was ready to sail.

It is my pleasure as well as duty here to thank the Norwegian whalers of South Georgia for their sympathy and help in our need. Among memories of kindness received in many lands sundered by the seas, the recollection of the hospitality and help given to me in South Georgia ranks high. There is a brotherhood of the sea. The men who go down to the sea in ships, serving and suffering, bring into their own horizons the perils of their brother sailormen.

McCarthy, McNeish and Vincent were landed on the Monday afternoon, and quickly began to show signs of increasing strength under a *régime* of warm quarters and abundant food. McCarthy looked woefully thin after he had emerged from a bath. He was over fifty years of age and the strain had told upon him more than upon the rest of us. The rescue came just in time for him.

At 9 AM on Tuesday morning the *Southern Sky* steamed out of the bay, while the whistles of the whaling station sounded a friendly farewell. On the Monday night we had foregathered aboard Captain Thom's ship with several whaling captains who were bringing up their sons to their own profession. They were "old stagers," with lined and seamed faces, and they were even more interested in the story of our voyage from Elephant Island than the younger generation was. It was pleasant to tell the tale to men who knew these sullen and treacherous southern seas, and they congratulated us on having accomplished a remarkable boat journey.

The early part of the voyage down to Elephant Island was uneventful. We made good progress, but the temperature fell very low, and the signs made me anxious about the chances of encountering ice. On the third night out the sea seemed to grow silent. The sea was freezing around us, and presently lumps of old pack began to appear among the new ice.

I realized that an advance through pack-ice was out of the question. The *Southern Sky* was a steel-built steamer and could not endure the blows of masses of ice. So I took the ship north, and at daylight on Friday we were clear of the pancake-ice. The morning of the 28th was dull and overcast, with little wind. Again the ship's head was turned to the southwest, but at 3 PM a definite line of pack showed up on the horizon. We were about seventy miles from Elephant Island, and we could not take the steamer through the ice which barred the way. Northwest we turned again. We were directly north of the island on the following day, and I made another move south. Heavy pack formed an impenetrable barrier.

To admit failure at this stage was hard, but facts had to be faced. The *Southern Sky* could not enter ice of even moderate thickness, the season was late, and we could not be sure that the ice would open for many months. The *Southern Sky* could only carry coal for ten days, and we had been out six days. We were 500 miles from the Falkland Islands and about 600 miles from South Georgia. So I determined that I would go to the Falklands, get a more suitable vessel either locally or from England, and make a second attempt to reach Elephant Island from that point.

After encountering very bad weather we arrived at Port Stanley, where the cable provided a link with the outer world, in the afternoon of May 31st. The harbormaster came out to meet us, and I went ashore to meet the Governor, Mr. Douglas Young, who offered me his assistance at once. He telephoned to Mr. Harding, the manager of the Falkland Island Station, and to my keen regret I learned that no ship of the required type was available at the islands.

That evening I cabled to His Majesty the King the first account of the loss of the *Endurance* and the subsequent adventures of the expedition. The next day I received the following message from the King:

> *Rejoice to hear of your safe arrival in the Falkland Islands and trust your comrades on Elephant Island may soon be rescued.*
>
> *George R. I.*

I will not attempt to describe in detail the events which followed our arrival at the Falkland Islands. Winter was advancing, and I was bent upon the rescue of my comrades at the earliest possible moment, for I was fully conscious that the lives of some of them might be the price of unnecessary delay.

A proposal to send a relief ship from England had been made, but she could not reach us for several weeks. In the meantime by wireless and cable I asked the governments of the South American Republics if they had any suitable ship which I could use for rescue. I wanted a wooden ship capable of pushing into loose ice, with fair speed and a reasonable coal capacity.

Messages of congratulations and goodwill were reaching me from all parts of the world, and the kindness of hundreds of friends was a very real comfort in a time of anxiety and stress.

The British Admiralty informed me that no suitable vessel was available in England, and that no relief could be expected before October. I replied that October would be too late. Then the British Minister in Montevideo telegraphed me regarding a trawler named *Instituto de Pesca* No. 1, belonging to the Uruguayan government. She was a stout little vessel, and the government had generously offered to equip her fully, and send her across to the Falkland Islands for me to take down to Elephant Island. Gladly I accepted this offer, and the trawler was in Port Stanley on June 10th. We started south at once.

The weather was bad but the trawler made good progress, and in the clear dawn of the third day we sighted the peaks of Elephant Island. Hope ran high; but our ancient enemy the pack was waiting for us, and within twenty miles of the island the trawler was stopped by an impenetrable barrier of ice. All our efforts to dodge or push through it were in vain. The island lay on our starboard quarter, but there was no possibility of approaching it.

The Uruguayan engineer reported to me that he had three days' coal left, and I had to give the order to turn back. A screen of fog hid the lower slopes of the island, and the men watching from the camp on the beach could not have seen the ship. When we reached Port Stanley with bunkers nearly empty and engines almost broken down, H. M. S. *Glasgow* was in the port and the British sailors welcomed us heartily as we steamed in.

The Uruguayan government offered to send the trawler to Punta Arenas and have her dry-docked there and made ready for another effort. But time was precious, and these preparations would have taken too long. I thanked the government then for its most generous offer, and want to say now that the kindness of the Uruguayans at this time earned my warmest gratitude. I ought also to mention the assistance given by Lieut. Ryan, a Naval Reserve officer, who navigated the ship to the Falklands, and came south on the attempt at relief. The *Instituto de Pesca* went off to Montevideo, and I looked round for another ship.

Opportunely a British mail-boat, the *Orita*, called at Port Stanley, and I boarded her with Worsley and Crean and crossed to Punta Arenas in the Magellan Straits. There the British Association of Magellanes took us to their hearts. Mr. Allan McDonald was especially prominent in his untiring efforts to assist in the rescue. He worked day and night, and it was mainly due to him that within three days they had raised a sum of £1,500 among themselves, chartered the schooner *Emma* and equipped her for our use. She was a forty-year-old oak schooner, strong and seaworthy, with an auxiliary oil engine.

Out of the complement of ten men all told who were manning the ship, there were eight different nationalities; but they were all good fellows and understood perfectly what was wanted. The Chilean government lent us a small steamer, the *Yelcho,* to tow us part of the way; but she could not touch ice, being built of steel. However, on July 12th we passed her our tow-rope and proceeded on our way. In bad weather we anchored next day, but, although the wind increased to a gale, I could delay no longer, so we hove up anchor in the early morning of the 14th. The strain on the tow-rope was too great. With the crack of a gun it broke.

Next day the gale continued, and the *Yelcho,* on my orders, returned to harbor. After three days of continuous bad weather we were left alone once more to try and rescue our comrades, about whom by this time I had very grave fears. At dawn of Friday, July 21st, we were were within 100 miles of the island, and we encountered the ice in the half-light. I waited for the full day and then tried to push through. The schooner was tossing like a cork in the swell, and after a few bumps I saw that she was actually lighter than the fragments of ice around her. Progress under such conditions was out of the question.

I worked the schooner out of the pack and stood to the east. We hove to for the night, which was now sixteen hours long. The winter was well advanced and the weather conditions were thoroughly bad. The ice to the southward was moving rapidly north. The motor engine had broken down and we were entirely dependent on the sails. We managed to make a little southing during the next day, but that night we lay off the ice in a gale, hove to, and morning found the schooner iced up. Some members of the scratch crew were played out by the cold and by the violent tossing.

I took the schooner south at every chance, but always the line of ice blocked the way. The engineer tried hard but could not keep the engines running, and the persistent south winds were dead ahead. It was hard to turn back a third time, but it had to be done. So we set a northerly course, and after a tempestuous passage once more reached Port Stanley. This was the third reverse, but I did not abandon my belief that the ice would not remain fast round Elephant Island during the winter, whatever the armchair experts at home might say.

We reached Port Stanley on August 8th, and I learned that the ship *Discovery* was to leave England at once and would reach the Falkland Islands about the middle of September. My good friend the Governor said that I could settle down at Port Stanley, and take things easily for a few weeks. But I could not be content to wait for six or seven weeks, knowing that 600 miles away my comrades were in desperate need. So I asked the Chilean government to send the *Yelcho* to take the schooner across to Punta Arenas, and they consented promptly, as they had to all my requests. So in a northwest gale we went across, narrowly escaping disaster on the way, and reached Punta Arenas on August 14th.

No suitable ship could be obtained, but the weather was improving, and I begged the Chilean government to let me have the *Yelcho* for a last attempt to reach the island. A small steel-built steamer, she was quite unsuitable for work in the pack, but I promised not to touch the ice. The government gave me another chance, and on August 25th I started south for the fourth attempt at relief.

This time Providence favored us. I found as we neared Elephant Island that the ice was open. A southerly gale had sent it northward temporarily, and the *Yelcho* had her chance to slip through. We approached the island in a thick fog, but I did not dare to wait for this to clear. At 10 AM on August 30th we passed some stranded bergs, then we saw the sea breaking on a reef, and I knew that we were just outside the island.

It was an anxious moment, for we had still to locate the camp and the pack could not be trusted to allow time for a prolonged search; but presently the fog lifted and revealed the cliffs and glaciers of Elephant Island. I proceeded to the east, and at 11:40 AM Worsley's keen eyes detected the camp, almost invisible under its covering of snow. The men ashore saw us at the same time, and we saw tiny black figures hurry to the beach and wave signals to us. We were about a mile and a half away from the camp.

I turned the *Yelcho* in, and within half an hour reached the beach with Crean and some of the Chilean sailors. I saw a little figure on a surf-beaten rock and recognized Wild. As I came nearer I called out, "Are you all well?" and he answered, "We are all well, Boss," and then I heard three cheers.

As I drew close to the rock I flung packets of cigarettes ashore; they fell on them like hungry tigers, for well I knew that for months tobacco had been dreamed and talked about. Some of the hands were in a rather bad way, but Wild had kept hope alive in their hearts. There was no time then to exchange news or congratulations. I did not even go up the beach to see the camp, which Wild assured me had been much improved.

A heavy sea was running, and a change of wind might bring the ice back at any time. I hurried the party aboard with all possible speed, taking also the records of the expedition and the essential portions of equipment. Everybody was aboard within an hour, and we steamed north at the *Yelcho's* best speed. The ice was still open, and nothing worse than an expanse of stormy ocean separated us from the South American coast.

During the run up to Punta Arenas I heard Wild's story, and blessed again the cheerfulness and resource which had served the party so well during four and a half months of privation. The twenty-two men were just at the end of their resources; but I will tell their tale in the succeeding chapter. Let me only say here that Wild had fought a magnificent fight against the demons of despondency and despair, which could but attack a party with only a precarious foothold between the grim ice fields and the treacherous, ice-strewn sea, and with only the scantiest stock of food.

The *Yelcho* had arrived at the right moment. Two days earlier she could not have reached the island, and a few hours later the pack might have been again impenetrable. We encountered bad weather on the way back to Punta Arenas, and the little ship labored heavily; but she had light hearts aboard. We entered the Straits of Magellan on September 3rd and reached Rio Secco at 8 AM. Two or three hours later we were at Punta Arenas, where we were given a welcome which we shall never forget. The Chilean people were no less enthusiastic than the British residents. The whole populace appeared to be in the streets. It was a great reception, and after the long, anxious months of strain we were in a mood to enjoy it.

During the next few weeks I received congratulations and messages of friendship from all over the world, and my heart went out to the good people who had remembered us in the press of terrible events on the battlefields. The Chilean government placed the *Yelcho* at my disposal to take the men up to Valparaiso and Santiago.

We reached Valparaiso on September 27th. Everything that could swim in the way of a boat was out to meet us, and at least thirty thousand people thronged the streets. On the following evening I lectured in Santiago for the British Red Cross and a Chilean Naval charity. The Chilean flag and the Union Jack were draped together. I saw the president and thanked him for the help he had given to a British expedition. His government had spent £4,000 on coal alone. In reply he recalled the part taken by British sailors in the making of the Chilean Navy.

The Chilean Railway Department provided a special train to take us across the Andes, and I proceeded to Montevideo in order personally to thank the president and government of Uruguay for their generous help. We were entertained royally at various spots en route. And then, after a brief call at Buenos Aires, we again crossed the Andes.

By this time I had made arrangements for the men and the staff to go to England, all hands being keen to take their places in the Empire's fighting forces. My own immediate task was the relief of the marooned Ross Sea party, and I decided to take Worsley with me. We hurried northwards *viâ* Panama, and at San Francisco caught a steamer which would get us to New Zealand at the end of November. I had been informed that the New Zealand government was arranging for the relief of the Ross Sea party, but my information was incomplete, and I was very anxious to be on the spot as quickly as possible.

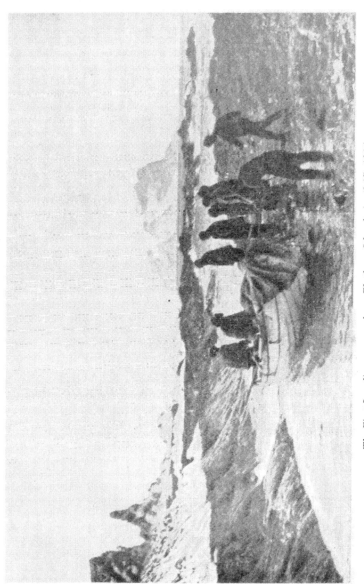

The First Landing ever made on Elephant Island; April 15, 1916

Hurley

Launching the James Caird

Hurley

Sea-elephants on South Georgia

Hurley

A Typical View in South Georgia

Hurley

One of the Glaciers we crossed

Hurley

Marooned on Elephant Island
The men under Wild in front of their hut

Greenstreet   McIlroy   Marston   Wordie   James   Holness   Stephenson   McLeod   Clark   Lees   Rickenson   Macklin

Green   Wild   Howe   Hudson   Cheetham   Bakewell   Hussey   Kerr

Hurley

"All safe! All well!" August 30th, 1916
"We tried to cheer, but excitement had gripped our vocal cords."

Hurley

Hurley

The Ross Sea Party

Mackintosh and Stenhouse in the center

CHAPTER SIXTEEN

ELEPHANT ISLAND

I HAVE OBTAINED AN ACCOUNT OF THE EXPERIENCES OF THE twenty-two men left behind on Elephant Island from their various diaries, supplemented by details obtained in conversation on the voyage back to civilization.

The first consideration, even more important than that of food, was to provide shelter, for several of the men were suffering severely from the ordeals through which they had passed. Rickenson, who bore up gamely to the last, collapsed from heart failure; Blackborrow and Hudson could not move. All were frostbitten in varying degrees.

The blizzard which sprang up on the day we landed at Cape Wild lasted for a fortnight; the tents, with the exception of the square tent occupied by Hurley, James and Hudson, were torn to ribbons. Sleeping bags and clothes were wringing wet, and the physical discomforts tended to produce acute mental depression. The two remaining boats had been turned upside down with one gunwale resting on the snow, and the other raised about two feet on rocks and cases, and under these the sailors, the invalids and some of the scientists at least found head-cover.

Shelter and warmth to dry their clothes was imperative, so Wild, who was left in command and in whom I had absolute confidence, hastened the excavation of the ice-cave in the slope, which had been started before I had left.

The high temperature, however, caused a continuous stream of water to drip from the roof and sides of the ice-cave, so Wild directed that big flat stones should be collected, and with these, two substantial walls, 4 feet high and 19 feet apart, were made.

> We are all ridiculously weak . . . stones that we could easily have lifted at other times we found quite beyond our capacity, and it needed two or three of us to carry some that would otherwise have been one man's load.

The site chosen for the hut was where the stove had been erected on the night of our arrival. It lay between two large boulders, which at least provided valuable protection from the wind, and further protection was provided to the north by Penguin Hill. As soon as the walls were completed and squared off, the two boats were laid upside down on them side by side. Their exact adjustment took some time, but was of paramount importance if our structure was to be the permanent affair we hoped it would be. Once in place they were securely chocked up and lashed down to the rocks. The few pieces of wood that we had were laid across from keel to keel, and over this the material of one of the torn tents was spread and secured with guys to the rocks. The walls were ingeniously contrived and fixed up by Marston. . . .

At last all was completed and we were invited to bring in our sodden bags, which had been lying out in the drizzling rain for hours; for the tents and boats that had previously sheltered them had all been requisitioned to form our new residence. We took our places under Wild's direction. There was no squabbling for best places, but it was noticeable that there was rather a rush for the billets up on the thwarts of the boat. Rickenson, who was still very weak and ill, but very cheery, obtained a place in the boat directly above the stove.

The floor was at first covered with snow and ice, frozen in among the pebbles, but this was cleared out, and the remainder of the tents spread out over the stones. Within the shelter of these cramped, but comparatively palatial, quarters, cheerfulness once more reigned among the party. Subsequently, when fine drift-snow forced its way through the crevices between the stones forming the end walls, Jaeger sleeping bags and coats were spread over the outside of these walls, packed over with snow and securely frozen up, and they effectively kept out the drift.

At first all the cooking was done outside under the lee of some rocks, further protection being provided by a wall of provision cases. There were two blubber stoves made from old oil drums, and one day, when the blizzard was unusually severe, an attempt was made to cook inside the hut. Pungent blubber-smoke, however, was the result of this first attempt, but a chimney, made by Kerr out of the tin lining of one of the biscuit cases, was soon fitted, and the smoke nuisance inside the hut was a thing of the past.

The cook and his assistant, which latter job was taken by each man in turn, were called about 7 AM, and breakfast was generally ready about 10 AM. Provision cases were then arranged in a wide circle round the stove, and those fortunate enough to be next it could dry their gear. So that all should benefit equally each man occupied his place at meal times for one day only, and moved up one on the succeeding day.

The great trouble in the hut was the absence of light. The canvas walls were covered with blubber-soot, and, with the snowdrifts accumulating round the hut, its inhabitants lived in a state of perpetual night. Wild was the first to overcome this difficulty by sewing the glass lid of a chronometer box into the canvas wall. Later on three other windows were added, and this enabled those men who were near enough to them to read and sew, which considerably relieved the monotony of the situation.

"Our reading material at this time consisted of two books of poetry, one book of *Nordenskjöld's Expedition,* one or two torn volumes of the *Encyclopædia Britannica,* and a penny cookery book, owned by Marston. Our clothes . . . had to be continually patched to keep them together at all."

The floor of the hut, having been raised by the addition of loads of clean pebbles, kept fairly dry during the cold weather, but when the temperature rose to just above freezing point the hut became the drainage-pool of all the surrounding hills. Wild noticed it first, when he found one morning that his sleeping bag was practically afloat.

Other men examined theirs with a like result, so bailing operations began forthwith. Hundreds of gallons of water had to be bailed out from the large hole which was dug in the floor. Eventually this watery problem was completely solved by removing a portion of one wall and digging a long channel nearly down to the sea.

A huge glacier across the bay behind the hut nearly put an end to the party. Enormous blocks of ice would break off and fall into the sea, the disturbance giving rise to great waves. One day Marston was outside the hut when a noise "like an artillery barrage" startled him. Looking up, he saw a tremendous wave, over 30 feet high, advancing rapidly across the bay, and threatening to sweep both the hut and its inhabitants into the sea. Fortunately, however, the loose ice which filled the bay damped the wave down so much that, though it flowed right under the hut, nothing was carried away. But it was a narrow escape, as nothing could have saved the men had they been washed into the sea.

Although they themselves gradually became accustomed to the darkness and dirt, extracts from their diaries show that they could still realize the conditions under which they were living.

"The hut grows more grimy everyday. Everything is sooty black. . . . It is at least comforting to feel that we can become no filthier. Our shingle floor will scarcely bear examination by strong light without causing even us to shudder and express our disapprobation at its state. . . . Such is our Home, Sweet Home."

"All joints are aching through being compelled to lie on the hard, rubbly floor which forms our bedsteads."

"Thank heaven man is an adaptable brute! If we dwell sufficiently long in this hut we are likely to alter our method of walking, for our ceiling, which is but 4 feet 6 inches high at its highest part, compels us to walk bent double or on all fours."

We are as regardless of our grime and dirt as is the Eskimo. We have been unable to wash since we left the ship, nearly ten months ago. For one thing we have no soap or towels; and, again, had we possessed these articles, our supply of fuel would only permit us to melt enough ice for drinking purposes. Had one washed, half a dozen others would have to go without a drink all day. One cannot suck ice to relieve the thirst, as at these low temperatures it cracks the lips and blisters the tongue. Still, we are all very cheerful.

During the whole of their stay on Elephant Island the weather was described by Wild as "simply appalling." On most days the air was full of snowdrift blown from the adjacent heights. On April 25th, the day after I left for South Georgia, the island was beset by heavy pack-ice, with snow and a wet mist. April ended with a terrific windstorm which nearly destroyed the hut. This lasted well into May, and a typical May day is thus described: "A day of terrific winds, threatening to dislodge our shelter. The wind is a succession of hurricane gusts that sweep down the glacier. Each gust heralds its approach by a low rumbling which increases to a thunderous roar. Snow, stones and gravel are flying about, and any gear left unweighted by very heavy stones is carried away to sea."

Heavy bales of sennegrass and boxes of cooking gear were lifted bodily in the air and carried away out of sight. These gusts often came without any warning, and on one occasion Hussey, who was outside digging up the day's meat, which had frozen to the ground, was very nearly blown into the sea. On rare occasions there were fine, calm, clear days, when the glow of the dying sun on the mountains and glaciers was incomparably beautiful.

About the middle of May a terrific blizzard sprang up, and Wild entertained grave fears for their hut. In this blizzard huge ice sheets, as big as windowpanes and about a quarter of an inch thick, were hurled about by the wind, making it as dangerous to walk about outside as if one were in an avalanche of splintered glass. Still, these winds from the south and southwest, though invariably accompanied by snow and low temperatures, were welcome, because they drove the pack-ice from the island, and so on each occasion gave rise to hopes of relief. Northeast winds, on the other hand, filled the bay with ice, and made it impossible for any ship to approach the island.

Thus the weather continued, alternating between southwest blizzards, when all hands were confined to the hut, and northeast winds which brought cold, damp, misty weather. Towards the end of July and beginning of August there were a few fine, calm days. Occasional glimpses of the sun were seen after the southwest winds had blown all the ice away, and the party, their spirits raised by Wild's unfailing optimism, again began to look eagerly for the rescue ship.

Unfortunately, however, the first three attempts to relieve the party coincided with the times when the island was beset by ice. From August 16th to August 27th the island was surrounded by pack-ice, but on the latter day a strong southwest wind drove all this ice from the bay, and, except for some stranded bergs, left a clear ice-free sea through which we finally made our way to Elephant Island.

Midwinter's Day, the great Polar festival, was duly observed. A "magnificent breakfast" of sledging ration hoosh, full strength, and well boiled to thicken it, with hot milk, was served. Luncheon consisted of a wonderful pudding, invented by Wild, and made of powdered biscuit boiled with twelve pieces of moldy nut-food. Supper was a very finely cut seal hoosh flavored with sugar. After supper they had a concert, accompanied by Hussey on his "indispensable banjo." The banjo was the last thing saved from the ship before she sank, and it was landed on Elephant Island practically unharmed, and did much to cheer the men. Nearly every Saturday night a concert was held.

The cook, who had carried on so well and for so long, was given a rest on August 9th, and as the cook and his "mate" had the privilege of scraping out the saucepans there was anxiety to secure the job. Food was getting terribly short, for the penguins and seals, which had migrated at the beginning of winter, had not yet returned, and old seal bones, which had been once used for a meal and thrown away, were dug up and stewed down with seawater. Penguin carcasses were likewise treated. One man wrote in his diary: "We had a sumptuous meal today—nearly five ounces of solid food each." No wonder, under the circumstances, that the thoughts and conversation of the party should turn to food.

It was largely due to Wild, and to his energy and resource, that the party kept cheerful all along, and, indeed, came out alive and so well. Assisted by the two surgeons, Drs. McIlroy and Macklin, he kept a watchful eye on the health of each man. His cheery optimism never failed, and each man in his diary speaks with admiration of him. I think without doubt that all the stranded party owe their lives to him. He more than justified the absolute confidence which I placed in him. Hussey, with his cheeriness and banjo, was another vital factor in chasing away symptoms of depression.

Once settled in the hut, the health of the party was, under the conditions, quite good. Everyone, of course, was rather weak, some were lightheaded, all were frostbitten, and others, later, had attacks of heart failure. Blackborrow, whose toes were so badly frostbitten in the boats, had to have all five amputated while on the island. That this operation, under the most difficult conditions, was very successful, speaks volumes for the skill and initiative of the surgeons. Hudson, who developed bronchitis and hip disease, was practically well when relief came. All the men were naturally weak when rescued, but all, thanks to Frank Wild, were alive and very cheerful.

August 30th, 1916, is described in their diaries as a "day of wonders." Food was very short, only two days' seal and penguin meat being left, and there was no prospect of any more. The whole party had been collecting limpets and seaweed to eat with the stewed seal bones. Lunch was being served by Wild; Hurley and Marston were waiting outside to take a last look at the direction from which they expected the ship to come.

From a fortnight after I had left, Wild had rolled up his sleeping bag each day with the remark, "Get your things ready, boys, the Boss may come today." And sure enough, one day, the mist opened and revealed the ship for which they had been waiting and longing for over four months.

Marston was the first to notice it, and immediately yelled out "Ship O!" Those in the hut mistook it for a call of "Lunch O!" so took no notice at first. Soon, however, we heard him pattering along the snow as fast as he could run, and, in a gasping voice, hoarse with excitement, he shouted, "Wild, there's a ship! Hadn't we better light a flare?" We all made one dive for our narrow door. Those who could not get through tore down the canvas walls in their hurry and excitement. The hoosh-pot, with our precious limpets and seaweed, was kicked over in the rush. There, just rounding the island which had previously hidden her from our sight, we saw a little ship flying the Chilean flag.

We tried to cheer, but excitement had gripped our vocal cords. Macklin had made a rush for the flagstaff, previously placed in the most conspicuous position on the ice slope. The running-gear would not work, and the flag was frozen into a solid mass, so he tied his jersey to the top of the pole for a signal.

Wild put a pick through our last remaining tin of petrol, and, soaking coats, mitts and socks with it, carried them to the top of Penguin Hill, and soon they were ablaze.

Meanwhile, most of us were on the foreshore watching anxiously for any signs that the ship had seen us, or for any answering signals. As we stood and gazed she seemed to turn away as if she had not seen us. Again and again we cheered, though our feeble cries could certainly not have carried so far. Suddenly she stopped, a boat was lowered, and we could recognize Sir Ernest's figure as he climbed down the ladder. Simultaneously we burst into a cheer, and then one said to the other, "Thank God, the Boss is safe." For I think that his safety was of more concern to us than our own.

Soon the boat was near enough for the Boss, who was standing up in the bows, to shout to Wild, "Are you all well?" To which he replied, "All safe, all well," and we could see a smile light up the Boss' face as he said, "Thank God."

Before he could land he threw ashore handfuls of cigarettes and tobacco, and these the smokers, who for two months had been trying to find solace in such substitutes as seaweed, finely chopped pipe-bowls, seal meat, and sennegrass, grasped greedily.

Blackborrow, who could not walk, had been carried to a high rock and propped up in his sleeping bag, so that he could view the wonderful scene.

Soon we were tumbling into the boat, and the Chilean sailors, laughing up at us, seemed as pleased at our rescue as we were. Twice more the boat returned, and within an hour of our first having sighted the boat we were heading northwards to the outer world, from which we had had no news for over twenty-two months.

We were like men awakened from a long sleep. We are trying to acquire suddenly the perspective which the rest of the world has acquired gradually through two years of war. . . .

Our first meal, owing to our weakness, proved disastrous to many of us, but we soon recovered. Our beds were shakedowns on cushions and settees, but I think we got very little sleep. It was just heavenly to lie and listen to the throb of the engines, instead of to the crack of the breaking floe, or the howling of the blizzard.

We intend to keep August 30th as a festival for the rest of our lives.

You can imagine my feelings, as I stood in the little cabin watching my rescued comrades eating the first good meal which had been offered to them for many, many months.

CHAPTER SEVENTEEN

THE ROSS SEA PARTY

I NOW TURN TO THE ROSS SEA PARTY AND THE *AURORA*. IN SPITE OF extraordinary difficulties, caused by the *Aurora* breaking out from her winter quarters before sufficient stores and equipment had been landed, Captain Æneas Mackintosh and the party under his command achieved the object of this side of the expedition. The depot, which was their main object, was laid in the spot indicated by me, and if the trans-continental party had been able to have crossed they would have found the assistance vital to the success of the undertaking.

Owing to the dearth of stores, clothing, and sledging equipment, the depot party was forced to travel more slowly and with greater difficulty than otherwise would have been the case. The result was that during this journey the finest qualities were called for, and the call was not in vain, as those who read the following pages will realize.

It is more than regrettable that, after so many months of hardship and toil, Mackintosh and Hayward should have been lost. Spencer-Smith, during those long days, suffering but never complaining, became an example to all men. Mackintosh and Hayward owed their lives on that journey to the care and strenuous endeavors of Joyce, Ernest Wild and Richards, who, also scurvy-stricken, but fitter than their comrades, dragged them on sledges through deep snow and blizzards.

I think that no more remarkable story of human endeavor has been revealed than the tale of that long march which I have collected from various diaries. Unfortunately the diary of the leader of this side of the expedition was lost with him. The outstanding feature of the Ross Sea side was the journey made by these six men. Mackintosh was fortunate for the long journey, in that he had these three men with him: Ernest Wild, Richards and Joyce.

Before relating the adventures of this party I want to emphasize my gratitude for the assistance I received both in Australia and New Zealand, especially in the latter dominion. And among many friends I wish to lay special stress on the names of Leonard Tripp, whose services to the expedition are beyond all praise, and of Edward Saunders. If ever a man had cause to be grateful for assistance in dark days, I am he.

The *Aurora,* under the command of Captain Æneas Mackintosh, sailed from Hobart for the Ross Sea on December 24th, 1914. The ship, if necessary, could spend two years in the Antarctic. My instructions, in brief, to Captain Mackintosh were to proceed to the Ross Sea, make a base at some convenient point in or near McMurdo Sound, land stores and equipment, and lay depots on the Great Ice Barrier in the direction of the Beardmore Glacier for the party I hoped to bring overland from the Weddell Sea coast.

The program involved some heavy sledging, but I had not anticipated that the work would be extremely difficult. The *Aurora* carried materials for a hut, full equipment for landing and sledging parties, stores and clothing of all the kinds required, and an ample supply of sledges. There were also dog teams and one of the motor-tractors. I told Captain Mackintosh to lay out depots to the south immediately after his arrival at his base, and directed him to place a depot of food and fuel oil at lat. 80° S. in 1914–15, with cairns and flags as guides to a sledging-party approaching from the direction of the Pole. In the 1915–16 season he would place depots further south.

The *Aurora* had an uneventful voyage southwards, and on Christmas Day anchored off the sealing-huts at Macquarie Island. The wireless station, erected by Sir Douglas Mawson's Australian Antarctic expedition, was still occupied, and the *Aurora* had some stores for the party living there. The *Aurora* sailed from the island on December 31st, and three days later they sighted the first iceberg, and on the following day the ship passed through the first belt of pack-ice. On January 7th Mount

Sabine, a mighty peak of the Admiralty Range, South Victoria Land, was sighted seventy-five miles distant.

It had been proposed that a party of three men should travel to Cape Crozier from winter quarters during the winter months to secure emperor penguins' eggs. The ship was to call at Cape Crozier, land provisions, and erect a small hut of fibro-concrete sheets for the use of this party. The ship was off the Cape on the afternoon of January 9th, and a boat was put off with a party to search for a landing place. But no place to land the hut and stores could be found.

Mackintosh then proceeded into McMurdo Sound, but, owing to heavy pack, it was not until January 16th that the ship reached a point off Cape Evans, where ten tons of coal and ninety-eight cases of oil were landed. During succeeding days the *Aurora* was worked southward, and by January 24th was within nine miles of Hut Point. There Mackintosh made the ship fast to sea-ice, then breaking up rapidly, and proceeded to arrange sledging-parties. He intended to direct the laying of the depots himself and to leave his first officer, Lieut. J. R. Stenhouse, in command of the *Aurora,* with instructions to select a base and land a party.

The first objective was Hut Point, where the hut erected by the *Discovery* expedition in 1902 stands. An advance party, consisting of Joyce (in charge), Jack and Gaze, with dogs and fully loaded sledges, left the ship on January 24th; Mackintosh, with Wild and Smith, followed the next day, and a supporting party of six men left the ship on January 30th. This last party consisted of Cope (in charge), Stevens, Ninnis, Hayward, Hooke and Richards.

These parties had a strenuous time during the following weeks. The men, fresh from shipboard, were not in the best of training, and the same was true of the dogs. It was unfortunate that the dogs had to be worked while they were still in poor condition and before they had learned to work together as teams. The result was the loss of many dogs, and this proved a most serious matter in the following season.

Captain Mackintosh and his party left the *Aurora* on the evening of January 25th. The dogs were full of eagerness after their long confinement aboard the ship, and Mackintosh hoped to reach Hut Point that night, but luck was against him. The weather broke after he had traveled about five miles, and snow, which completely obscured all landmarks, sent him into camp on the sea-ice. On January 27th, after missing their way in the thick weather, the party reached Hut Point at 4 PM. There Mackintosh found a note from Joyce who had been at the Hut on the 25th. The Hut contained some stores left there by earlier expeditions.

The party stayed at the Hut for the night, and Mackintosh left a note for Stenhouse, directing him to place provisions there, in case the sledging parties did not return in time to be taken off by the ship. Early next morning Joyce reached the Hut. He had met bad ice and had returned to consult Mackintosh about the route to be followed. Mackintosh directed him to steer out towards Black Island in crossing the head of the Sound beyond Hut Point.

Mackintosh left Hut Point on January 28th, with a sledge weighing 1,200 lb. This was a heavy load, but the dogs were pulling well, and he thought it practicable. Difficulties from soft snow and the fact that the dogs soon ceased to pull cheerfully began almost at once. The distance covered in the day was under four miles.

A fall of snow held up the party through the following day, and, owing to the soft surface, Mackintosh decided to travel by night. They left the camp before midnight, but difficulties again beset them. "Try as we would, no movement could be produced. Reluctantly we unloaded and began the tedious task of relaying." The work was terrific, and, after struggling for four hours, they camped to wait for evening, when they hoped the surface would be better. "I must say," Mackintosh wrote, "I feel somewhat despondent, as we are not getting on as well as I expected, nor do we find it as easy as one would gather from reading."

The two parties met again that day. Joyce also had been compelled to relay his load, and all hands labored strenuously and advanced slowly. They reached the edge of the Barrier on the night of January 30th. The dogs were showing signs of fatigue, and when they camped at 6:30 AM on January 31st, Mackintosh reckoned that the distance covered in twelve and a half hours was about two and a half miles. The experiences of the party during the following day can be shown by extracts from Mackintosh's diary.

"Sunday, January 31st. Started off this afternoon at 3 PM. Surface too dreadful for words. We sink into snow at times up to our knees, the dogs struggling out of it, panting and making great efforts. After proceeding about 1,000 yards I spotted some poles. We shaped course for these and found Captain Scott's Safety Camp. After lunching we dug round the poles, and, after getting down about 3 feet, we found a bag of oats and two cases of dog biscuit. A good find. About forty paces away we found a venesta-lid sticking out of the snow. Smith scraped round this with his ice axe, and presently found one of the motor sledges used by Captain Scott. Everything was just as it had been left, the petrol tank partly filled and apparently unharmed."

"February 1st. After lunch we decided, as the surface was improving, to make a shot at traveling with the whole load. It was a backbreaking job. The great trouble is to get the sledge started after the many unavoidable stops. We managed to cover one mile. Even this is better than relaying. We then camped—the dogs being entirely done up, poor brutes."

"February 2nd. We were awakened this afternoon by hearing Joyce's dogs barking. They have done well and have caught us up. We issued a challenge to race him to the Bluff, which he accepted. When we turned out at 6:30 PM his camp was seen about three miles ahead, and we reached it by 1 AM. The dogs, seeing the camp ahead, had been pulling well, but when we arrived off it they were not inclined to go on. This starting business is terrible work. If the dogs do not pull together we cannot move. Sledging is real hard work; but we are getting along."

During the next few days the surface improved and better progress was made. Joyce was traveling by day and Mackintosh by night, so that the parties passed one another daily on the march. A blizzard on February 10th confined the parties to their tents for twenty-four hours. On the morning of the next day the weather moderated, and Mackintosh camped beside Joyce and proceeded to rearrange the parties.

He decided to take the best dogs from the two teams and continue the march with Joyce and Wild, while Smith, Jack and Gaze went back to Hut Point with the remaining dogs. This involved the adjustment of sledge-loads, so that proper supplies might be available for the depots. Mackintosh had eight dogs and Smith had five. A depot of oil and fuel was laid at this point and marked by a cairn with a bamboo pole rising 10 feet above it.

The change made for better progress. Smith turned back at once, and the other party went ahead fairly rapidly. They built a cairn of snow after each hour's traveling to serve as guides to the depot and as marks for the return journey. During succeeding days the party plodded forward, covering from five to twelve miles a day, according to the surface and weather, building cairns regularly, and checking their route by taking bearings of the mountains to the west. On February 21st Mackintosh wrote: "The temperature was very low this morning, and handling the theodolite was not too warm a job for the fingers. My whiskers froze to the metal while I was taking a sight."

They had reached lat. 80° S., and there they laid a depot. The stores were placed in a cairn built to a height of 8 feet, and on the top they placed a bamboo pole with a flag. Smaller cairns were built at right angles to the depot as a guide to the overland party. "Tomorrow we hope to lay out cairns to the westward, and then to shape our course for the Bluff."

But owing to a blizzard it was not until the afternoon of the 23rd that Mackintosh and Joyce tried to lay out cairns to the west. Two dogs had died during the storm, and after marching a mile and a half to the westward and building a cairn, the weather became so thick that they thought it unwise to proceed further. So they returned to the camp, and on the morning of February 24th, with snow still falling, they started the return march; but they had only gone 400 yards when thick fog compelled them again to pitch their tent.

"We are going back with only ten days' provisions, so it means pushing on for all we are worth. These stoppages are truly annoying. The poor dogs are feeling hungry; they eat their harness or any straps that may be about. If we had not been so delayed we might have been able to give them a good feed at the Bluff depot, but now that is impossible."

The experiences of the next few days were unhappy. Another blizzard brought heavy snow and held the party up throughout the 25th and 26th.

"Outside is a scene of chaos. We long to be off, but the howl of the wind shows how impossible it is. I am afraid that the dogs will not pull through. We have a week's provisions and 160 miles to travel. It appears that we will have to get another week's provisions from the depot, but don't wish it. Will see what luck tomorrow. Of course, at Bluff we can replenish."

A day later Mackintosh continued: "We are now reduced to one meal in twenty-four hours. It is a rotten, miserable time. It is bad enough to wait, but we have also the wretched thought of having to use the provisions already depoted, for which we have had this hard struggle."

The weather cleared on the 27th, and Mackintosh and Joyce had to return to the depot and secure some provisions. On the following morning the party resumed the homeward journey, and made good progress. But the dogs had reached almost the limit of their endurance; three of them fell out, unable to work longer, while on the march, and on March 2nd the remaining dogs collapsed. "They are all lying down in our tracks. They have a painless death, for they curl up in the snow and fall into a sleep from which they will never wake."

On March 3rd the party made only three and a half miles. They found the sledge exceedingly heavy to pull, and Mackintosh decided to remove the outer runners and scrape the bottom. He also left behind all spare gear, and found the lighter sledge easier to pull. On the 5th he wrote, "We are struggling along at a mile an hour. It is a very hard pull, the surface being very sticky."

The conditions altered during the next day when a southerly wind made it possible to use a sail. But the handling of the ropes and sail caused many frostbites, and occasionally the men were dragged along the surface by the sledge. During the night the wind increased, and by the morning of the 7th was blowing with blizzard force. The party could not move again until the 8th. They were still finding the sledge very heavy and were disappointed at their slow progress, their marches being six to eight miles a day.

On the 10th they got the Bluff Peak in line with Mount Discovery. My instructions had been that the Bluff depot should be laid on this line, and as the depot had been placed north of the line on the outward journey, owing to thick weather making it impossible to pick up the landmarks, Mackintosh now meant to move the stores to the proper place. He pitched camp at the new depot site, and went across, with Joyce and Wild, to the depot flag, about four miles away, and found the stores as he had left them. These stores were successfully transferred to the correct site, and after a day's blizzard the weather was fine on March 12th, and they built a cairn for the depot. Early in the afternoon they resumed their march northwards and made three miles before camping.

"Our bags," Mackintosh wrote that night, "are getting into a bad state, as it is some time now since we have had an opportunity to dry them. Getting away in the mornings is our bitterest time. The putting on of the finneskoe is a nightmare, for they are always frozen stiff, and we have a great struggle to force our feet into them. We are miserable until we are actually on the move, then warmth returns with the work."

Owing to blizzards the march could not be resumed until March 15th. By this time food was again short, and both Joyce and Wild had toes frostbitten while in their bags, and found difficulty in restoring the circulation. Wild suffered particularly in this way.

"March 15th. The air temperature this morning was –35° Fahr. Last night was one of the worst I have ever experienced. To cap everything I developed toothache and was in positive agony. Joyce and Wild both had a bad night, their feet giving them trouble. We have had to reduce our daily ration. Frostbites are frequent in consequence. The surface became very rough in the afternoon and the light also was bad. We are continually falling, for we are unable to distinguish the high and low parts of the surface. Our matches, among other things, are running short, and we have given up using them except for lighting the Primus."

The party found the light bad again the next day, and made fairly good progress, and on the evening of March 19th they camped abreast of "Corner Camp," where they had been on February 1st. But on the following day they turned towards Castle Rock and proceeded across the disturbed area where the Barrier impinges upon the land. Joyce put his foot through the snow covering of a fairly large crevasse, and the course had to be changed to avoid this danger. The march for the day was only two miles 900 yards, but, although Mackintosh felt the pace was too slow, the bad surface prevented him from quickening it. The food had been cut down nearly to half rations, and at this reduced rate the supply would be finished in two days. "The first thought this morning was that we must do a good march," Mackintosh wrote on March 22ⁿᵈ. "Once we can get to Safety Camp we are right. We have managed quite a respectable forenoon march. We had lunch at 1 PM, and then had left over one meal at full rations and a small quantity of biscuits. After lunch we again accomplished a good march, the wind favoring us for two hours. We are anxiously looking out for Safety Camp."

The morning of March 23ʳᵈ found them prisoners. A blizzard with drift had sprung up, and the weather was appalling. "This weather is rather alarming, for if it continues we are in a bad way. We have just made a meal of cocoa mixed with biscuit-crumbs. This has warmed us up a little, but on empty stomachs the cold is penetrating."

Later in the afternoon the weather cleared, but too late for the men to move on that day. They made a start at 7 AM on the 24ᵗʰ.

We have some biscuit-crumbs in the bag and that is all. Our start was made under most bitter circumstances, all of us being attacked by frostbites. Wild is a mass of bites, and we are all in a bad way. We had been pulling about two hours when Joyce's smart eyes picked up a flag. We shoved on for all we were worth, and as we got closer, sure enough, the cases of provisions loomed up. Soon we were putting our gastronomic capabilities to the test. While Wild was getting the Primus lighted he called out to us that he believed his ear had gone. This was the last piece of his face left whole—nose, cheeks and neck all having bites. The ear was a pale green, but I quickly put the palm of my hand to it and brought it round. Then his fingers went, and to bring back the circulation he put them over the lighted Primus, a terrible thing to do. As a result he was in agony.

Soon the hot hoosh sent warmth tingling through us. We felt like new beings. We simply ate till we were full, mug after mug. Then we replaced the cases we had pulled down from the depot, and proceeded towards the Gap. Just before leaving

Joyce discovered a note left by Spencer-Smith and Richards. This told us that both the other parties had returned to the Hut, and apparently all was well. So that is good.

By 7 PM the party had failed to find a suitable place to descend to the sea-ice, so they camped, hoping to reach Hut Point on the morrow. They broke camp on the morning of March 25th, with the thermometer recording 55° of frost, and a short time later they arrived at Hut Point and reached the door of the Hut. "We shouted. No sound. Shouted again and presently a dark object appeared. This turned out to be Cope, who was by himself. We heard then how the ship had called here on March 11th and picked up Spencer-Smith, Richards, Ninnis, Hooke and Gaze, the present members here being Cope, Hayward and Jack. I got a letter here from Stenhouse giving a summary of his doings since we left him. The ship's party also have not had a very rosy time."

The six men now at Hut Point were cut off from the winter quarters of the expedition at Cape Evans by the open water of McMurdo Sound. Naturally Mackintosh was anxious to get in touch with the ship and the other members of the shore party; but he could not move until the sea-ice was firm, and, as events occurred, he did not reach Cape Evans until the beginning of June. At the Hut he and his companions lived an uneventful life under primitive conditions. Mackintosh records that the members of the party were contented enough, but, owing largely to the soot and grease from the blubber-stove, unspeakably dirty. The store of seal-blubber ran low early in April, but on April 15th several seals were killed. The operations of killing and skinning them made worse the blackened and greasy clothes of the men.

CHAPTER EIGHTEEN

WINTERING IN McMurdo Sound

THE *AURORA*, AFTER PICKING UP SIX MEN AT HUT POINT ON MARCH 11th, had gone back to Cape Evans. The position chosen for the winter quarters of the ship was at Cape Evans, immediately off the hut erected by Captain Scott on his last expedition. The ship on March 14th lay about forty yards offshore, bows seaward. The final moorings were six hawsers and one cable astern, made fast to the shore anchors, and two anchors with about seventy fathoms of cable out forward.

On March 23rd Mr. Stenhouse landed a party consisting of Stevens, Spencer-Smith, Gaze and Richards, and these four men took up their quarters in Captain Scott's hut. They had been instructed to kill seals for meat and blubber, and carry out routine observations. The landing of stores, gear and coal did not proceed at all rapidly, it being assumed that the ship would remain at her moorings through the winter. Some tons of coal were landed during April, but most of it stayed on the beach, and much of it was lost later when the sea-ice went out.

This shore party was in the charge of Stevens, and his report, handed to me much later, gives a succinct account of what occurred, from the point of view of the men at the hut. I quote from it very briefly:

Cape Evans, Ross Island,
July 30th, 1915
On March 23rd, 1915, a party consisting of Spencer-Smith, Richards
and Gaze was landed at Cape Evans Hut in my charge. Spencer-Smith

134

received instructions to devote his time exclusively to photography. I was verbally instructed that the main duty of the party was to obtain a supply of seals for food and fuel. Scientific work was also to be carried on.

Meteorological instruments were at once installed. . . . The whole of the time of the scientific members of the party was occupied. All seals seen were secured.

In general the weather was unsettled, blizzards occurring frequently and interrupting communication with the ship across the ice. Only small, indispensable supplies of stores and no clothes were issued to the party on shore. Only part of the scientific equipment was able to be transferred to the shore, and the necessity to obtain that prevented some members of the party landing all their personal gear.

Though, I believe, it was considered on board that the ship was secure, there was still considerable anxiety felt. The anchors had held badly before, and the power of the ice pressure on the ship was uncomfortably obvious. . . .

On May 6ᵗʰ the ice was in and people passed freely between the shore and the ship. At 11 PM the wind was south, backing to southeast, and blew at forty miles an hour. The ship was still in her place. At 3 AM on the 7ᵗʰ the wind had not increased to any extent, but ice and ship had gone. As she was not seen to go we are unable to say whether the vessel was damaged. . . . On the afternoon of the 7ᵗʰ the weather cleared somewhat, but nothing was seen of the ship. . . . Nothing has since been seen or heard of the ship, though a lookout was kept.

Immediately the ship went as accurate an inventory as possible of all stores ashore was made, and the rate of consumption of foodstuffs so regulated that they would last ten men for not less than one hundred weeks. Coal and meat were very short, and were therefore used as carefully as possible.

A. Stevens

The men ashore did not at once abandon hope of the ship returning before the Sound froze firmly, but when the most violent blizzard yet experienced by the party began on May 10ᵗʰ, hope grew slender. This gale lasted for three days, the wind attaining a velocity of seventy miles an hour. The shore party took a gloomy view of the ship's chances of safety among the ice-floes of the Ross Sea under such conditions.

Stevens and his companions made a careful survey of their position and realized the serious difficulties ahead of them. No general provisions and no clothing required for sledging had been landed. Much of the sledging gear was also aboard. Fortunately the hut contained both food and clothing, left there by Captain Scott's expedition. As many seals as possible were killed and the meat and blubber were stored.

June 2ⁿᵈ brought a welcome addition to the party in the men who had been forced to remain at Hut Point until the sea-ice was firm. There were now ten men at Cape Evans—namely, Mackintosh, Spencer-Smith, Joyce, Wild, Cope, Stevens, Hayward, Gaze, Jack and Richards. The winter had closed down upon the Antarctic and no move could be made before the beginning of September. Meanwhile they overhauled the available stores and gears, made plans for the future, and lived the severe, but not altogether unhappy, life of the polar explorer in winter quarters.

Mackintosh, writing on June 5ᵗʰ, surveyed his position:

> The decision of Stenhouse to make this bay the wintering place of the ship was not reached without much thought and consideration of all eventualities. He had already tried the Glacier Tongue and other places, but at each of them the ship had been in an exposed and dangerous position. When this bay was tried the ship withstood several blizzards. . . . Taking everything into account, it was quite a fair judgment on his part to assume that the ship would be secure here. . . . The accident proved again the uncertainty of conditions in these regions.

The *Aurora* could have found safe winter quarters farther up McMurdo Sound, but would have run the risk of being frozen in over the following summer, and I had given instructions to Mackintosh before he went south that this danger must be avoided.

Mackintosh continued:

> Meanwhile we are preparing here for a prolonged stay. The shortage of clothing is our principal hardship. The members of the party from Hut Point have the clothes we wore when we

left the ship on January 25th. I cannot imagine a dirtier set of people. . . . All is working smoothly here, and everyone is taking the situation very philosophically.

Stevens is in charge of the scientific staff and is now the senior officer ashore. Joyce is in charge of the equipment and has undertaken to improvise clothes from what canvas we can find here. Wild is working with Joyce. He is a cheerful, willing soul. Richards has taken over the keeping of the meteorological log. He is a young Australian, a hard, conscientious worker, and I look for good results from his endeavors. Jack, another young Australian, is his assistant. Hayward is the handy man, and responsible for the supply of blubber. Gaze, another Australian, is working with Hayward. Spencer-Smith, the *padre*, is in charge of photography, and, of course, assists in the general routine work. Cope is the medical officer. . . .

The day after my arrival I explained the necessity for economy in the use of fuel, light and stores, in view of the possibility that we may have to stay here for two years. . . . We are not going to begin work for the sledging operations until we know more definitely the fate of the *Aurora*. I dare not think any disaster has occurred.

During the remaining days of June the men washed and mended clothes, killed seals, made minor excursions, and discussed plans for the future. They had six dogs, and the animals were well-fed and carefully tended. The party was anxious to visit Cape Royds, north of Cape Evans, but at the end of June open water remained right across the Sound and a crossing was impossible. At Cape Royds is the hut used by the Shackleton expedition of 1907–1909, and the stores and supplies it contains would have been very useful.

During July Mackintosh made several trips northwards on the sea-ice, but always found that he could not get far. The improving light told of the returning sun, and stores were being weighed out in readiness for the sledging expeditions. Blizzards were frequent and persistent.

On August 12th a small fire broke out in the hut. The acetylene-gas lighting plant installed in the hut by Captain Scott had been rigged, and one day it developed a leak. One of the party searched for the leak with a lighted candle, and an explosion fired some woodwork, but fortunately the outbreak was quickly extinguished. The loss of the hut at this stage would have been a tragic incident.

On August 13th Mackintosh and Stevens paid a visit to Cape Royds. They decided to attempt the journey over the Barne Glacier, and, after crossing a crevassed area, they got to the slopes of Cape Barne and thence down to the sea-ice. This ice was strong enough for their purpose, and they soon reached the Cape Royds hut.

"The outer door of the hut we found to be off," Mackintosh wrote.

A little snow had drifted into the porch, but this was soon cleared away. We then entered, and in the center of the hut found a pile of snow and ice, which had come through the open ventilator in the roof. We soon closed this. Stevens prepared a meal while I cleared the ice and snow away with a shovel, which we found outside.

After our meal we began to take an inventory of the stores inside. Tobacco was our first thought. Of this we found one tin of Navy Cut and a box of cigars. Soap, too, which ensures us a wash and clean clothes when we get back. . . . Over the stove in a conspicuous place we found a notice left by Scott's party that parties using the hut should leave the dishes clean.

Mackintosh and Stevens stayed at the hut over the next day and thoroughly examined the stores there. Outside the hut they found a pile of cases containing meats, flour, dried vegetables and sundries, at least a year's supply for a party of six. They found no new clothing, but collected some worn garments which could be made serviceable. On August 15th they set out, carrying their load of spoils, and soon reached Cape Evans. A blizzard raged on the next day, and Mackintosh congratulated himself on having chosen such a fortunate time for the trip.

The record of the remaining part of August is not eventful. All hands were making preparations for the sledging and were rejoicing in the increasing daylight. The sledging of stores to Hut Point, in preparation for the depot-laying journeys on the Barrier, was to begin on September 1st. Before that date Mackintosh discussed plans fully with the members of his party. Stores, he considered, were sufficient, but the supply of clothes and tents was more difficult. Three tents were available, a sound one landed from the *Aurora,* and two old ones left by Captain Scott. Garments brought from the ship could be supplemented by old clothing found at Hut Point and Cape Evans. Mackintosh had enough sledges, but there were only four useful dogs left. They did not make a full team, and could merely be used as an auxiliary to manhaulage.

The scheme adopted by Mackintosh, after discussion, was that nine men, divided into three parties of three each, should undertake the sledging. One man was to be left at Cape Evans to continue the meteorological observations during the summer. Mackintosh estimated that the provisions required for the consumption of the depot parties, and for the depots to be placed southward to the foot of the Beardmore Glacier, would amount to 4,000 lb. The first depot was to be placed off Minna Bluff, and from there southward a depot was to be placed on each degree of latitude. The final depot would be at the foot of the Beardmore Glacier. The initial task would be the haulage of stores from Cape Evans to Hut Point—thirteen miles. All the sledging stores had to be taken across, and Mackintosh proposed to place additional supplies there in case a party, returning late from the Barrier, had to spend winter months at Hut Point.

The first party, consisting of Mackintosh, Richards and Spencer-Smith, left Cape Evans on September 1st with 600 lb. of stores on one sledge, and had an uneventful journey to Hut Point. They pitched a tent halfway across the bay, on the sea-ice, and left it there to be used by various parties during the month. The second trip to Hut Point was made by nine men, with three sledges, and eight men made the third journey. This last party proceeded from Hut Point the next day (September 4th) with loaded sledges to Safety Camp, on the edge of the Barrier. This camp would be the starting-point for the march over the Barrier to the Minna Bluff depot.

"Everybody is up to his eyes in work," runs the last entry in the journal left by Mackintosh at Cape Evans.

All gear is being overhauled, and personal clothing is having the last stitches. We have been improvising shoes to replace the finniskoe, of which we are badly short. Tomorrow (October 1st) we start for Hut Point. Gaze, who is suffering from bad feet, is remaining behind and will probably be relieved by Stevens after our first trip. With us we take three months' provisions to leave at Hut Point.

The nine men reached Hut Point on October 1st. They took the last loads with them. Three sledges and three tents were to be taken on to the Barrier, and the parties were as follows: No. 1: Mackintosh, Spencer-Smith and Wild; No. 2: Joyce, Cope and Richards; No. 3: Jack, Hayward and Gaze. On October 3rd and 4th some stores left at Halfway Camp were brought in, and other stores were moved on to Safety Camp. Bad weather delayed the start of the depot-laying expedition until October 9th.

→ CHAPTER NINETEEN ←

LAYING THE DEPOTS

MACKINTOSH'S ACCOUNT OF THE DEPOT-LAYING JOURNEYS OF HIS parties in the summer of 1915–16 unfortunately is not available. He kept a diary, but he had it with him when he was lost on the sea-ice in the following winter. This short narrative of the journeys is compiled from notes kept by Joyce, Richards and others, and I may say here that it is a record of dogged endeavor in the face of great difficulties and serious dangers.

It is always easy to be wise after the event, and one may realize now that the use of the dogs before they were in condition and trained was a mistake. In consequence hardly any dogs were available for the more important journeys of 1915–16. For six months the men were sledging almost continuously; they suffered from frostbite, scurvy, snow blindness, and utter weariness of overtaxed bodies. But they placed the depots in the required positions, and had the Weddell Sea party been able to cross the Antarctic continent, stores and fuel would have been waiting for us where we expected to find them.

On October 9th the position was that the nine men at Hut Point had with them the stores required for the depots and for their own maintenance through the summer. The remaining dogs were at Cape Evans. A small quantity of stores had already been conveyed to Safety Camp on the edge of the Barrier beyond Hut Point. Mackintosh intended to form a large depot off Minna Bluff, seventy miles out from Hut Point, and this would require several trips with heavy loads.

Then he would use the Bluff depot as a base for the journey to Mount
Hope, at the foot of the Beardmore Glacier, where the final depot
was to be laid.

The party left Hut Point on the morning of October 9th, the nine
men hauling on one rope and trailing three loaded sledges. They
reached Safety Camp in the early afternoon, and, after repacking the
sledges with a load of about 2,000 lb., they began the journey over
the Barrier. Pulling proved very difficult, and next day it was decided
to separate the sledges, three men to each sledge. The new arrangement was not a success, owing to differences in hauling capacity and
inequalities in the loading of sledges. So on the morning of the 12th,
Mackintosh decided to push forward with Wild and Spencer-Smith,
hauling one sledge with a relatively light load, and leave Joyce and the
remaining five to bring two sledges and the rest of the stores at their
best pace. This arrangement was maintained on the later journeys.

Persistent head winds with occasional drift made the conditions
unpleasant and caused many frostbites, but Joyce's party reached the
Bluff depot on the evening of the 21st and found that Mackintosh
had been there on the 19th. Mackintosh had left 178 lb. of provisions,
and Joyce left one sledge and 273 lb. of stores. The most interesting
incident of the return journey was the discovery of a note left by
Mr. Cherry-Garrard for Captain Scott on March 19th, 1912, only a few
days before Captain Scott perished at his camp farther south. Joyce
reached the hut in a blizzard on the night of the 27th, and found that
Mackintosh and his party had arrived three days before. Gaze had
also arrived with the dogs.

On the second journey to the Bluff depot Mackintosh decided to
use the dogs, and this plan involved sending a party to Cape Evans
to get dog-pemmican. Mackintosh himself, with Wild and Spencer-
Smith, started south again. Joyce remained in charge at Hut Point
with instructions to start south directly the dog food was obtained.
Stevens now took Gaze's place at the base, and the party, after being
delayed by a blizzard, got away from Hut Point on November 5th. The
men pulled in harness with the four dogs, and, as the surface was soft
and the loads on the two sledges heavy, the advance was slow. Joyce,
however, reached the Bluff depot on the evening of the 14th and left

624 lb. of provisions. Mackintosh had been there several days earlier and had left 188 lb. of stores.

Six days later Joyce was back again after an adventurous finish to his journey. About 10:30 AM on this day (November 20th) the party encountered heavy pressure-ice with crevasses, and had many narrow escapes. "After lunch," Joyce wrote, "we came on four crevasses quite suddenly. Jack fell through. We could not alter course, or else we should have been steering among them, so galloped right across. We were going so fast that the dogs which went through were jerked out."

On the 25th the men were again fit enough to start on their third journey to the Bluff. Mackintosh was some distance ahead, but the two parties met on the 28th and discussed plans. Mackintosh was proceeding to the Bluff depot with the intention of taking stores to the depot placed on lat. 80° S. in the first season's sledging. Joyce, after depositing his third load at the Bluff was to return to Hut Point for the last load, and the parties then were to join forces for the journey southward to Mount Hope.

Joyce was back again at Hut Point by December 7th, and, after resting dogs and men, started off once more on December 13th. This was the worst journey the party had made. Crevasses and blizzards caused infinite trouble, but they reached Bluff depot on December 28th and found that Mackintosh had gone south two days before on his way to the 80° S. depot, but he had not made much progress and his camp was in sight. He had left instructions to Joyce to follow him.

Joyce left the Bluff depot on December 29th, and the parties were together two days later. Mackintosh handed Joyce instructions to proceed with his party to lat. 81° S., and place a depot there. He was then to send three men back to Hut Point, and proceed to lat. 82° S., where he would lay another depot. Then if provisions permitted he would push south as far as lat. 83°. Mackintosh himself was reinforcing the depot at lat. 80° S. and would then carry on southward.

The next important incident was the appearance of a defect in one of the two Primus lamps used by Joyce's party, since it was impossible to travel without the means of melting snow and preparing hot hoosh. Joyce, therefore, decided to send three men back from the 80° S. depot, which he reached on January 6th, 1916. Cope, Gaze and Jack returned and reached Cape Evans on January 16th. Joyce, Richards and Hayward went forward with a load of 1,280 lb., building cairns at short intervals as guides to the depots. The dogs were being very well fed and Joyce wrote: "It is worth it for the wonderful amount of work they are doing. If we can keep them to 82° S. I can honestly say it is through their work we have got through."

On January 8th Mackintosh joined Joyce, and from that point the parties, six men strong, went forward together. On the evening of the 12th they reached lat. 81° S., and built a large cairn for the depot. Some of the marching had been done in thick weather, but by means of frequent cairns, with a scrap of black cloth on top of each one, they had managed to keep their course.

The party moved southwards again on January 13th in bad weather. "It was really surprising to find how we got on in spite of the snow and pie-crust surface. The dogs are doing splendidly. The distance for the day was ten miles 720 yards; a splendid performance considering surface and weather." During succeeding days they advanced rapidly, the daily distances being from ten to twelve miles, and they reached lat. 82° S. on the morning of January 18th. Mackintosh was in trouble with the Primus lamp in his tent, and this made it inadvisable again to divide the party.

It was, therefore, decided that all should proceed and that the last depot should be placed on the base of Mount Hope, at the foot of the Beardmore Glacier, in lat. 83° 30′ S. The party proceeded at once and advanced five miles beyond the depot before camping on the evening of the 18th.

The sledge loads, relieved of the stores deposited at the various depots, were now comparatively light, and on the 19th a good advance was made. But new troubles were developing. Spencer-Smith was suffering from swollen and painful legs and Mackintosh was showing signs of exhaustion. A mountain, believed to be Mount Hope, could be seen ahead, over thirty miles away.

Spencer-Smith, who had struggled on gamely, started next morning and kept going until noon. Then he reported his inability to proceed, and Mackintosh called a halt. Spencer-Smith suggested that he should be left with provisions and a tent while the others pushed on to Mount Hope, and pluckily assured Mackintosh that the rest would put him right. This plan, after consultation, was agreed to, Mackintosh feeling that the depot must be laid and that delay was dangerous. Spencer-Smith was left with a tent, a sledge and provisions, and told to expect the returning party in about a week. Everything possible to make him comfortable was done. He bade his companions a cheery "Goodbye" after lunch, and before evening the party was six or seven miles away.

Foggy weather hindered the advance, but on the 25th the party did seventeen and three-quarter miles, and camped on the edge of the "biggest ice-pressure" Joyce had ever seen. Of the work done on the 26th Joyce wrote, "Skipper, Richards and myself, roped ourselves together, I taking the lead, to try and find a course through this pressure. We came across very wide crevasses, went down several, came on top of a very high ridge, and such a scene! Imagine thousands of tons of ice churned up to a depth of about 300 feet." But in spite of all difficulties the depot was laid. On the return journey Joyce was attacked by snow blindness but "still pulled his whack," and on the 29th they reached Spencer-Smith's camp, and found him in his sleeping bag and quite unable to walk. Joyce's diary of this date refers rather gloomily to the outlook, for he guessed that Mackintosh also would be unable to make the homeward march. "The dogs," he added, "are still keeping fit. If they will only last to 80° S. we shall then have enough food to take them in, and then if the ship is in I guarantee they will live in comfort the remainder of their lives."

No march, owing to a blizzard, could be made on the 30th, but eight miles were made on the 31st, with Spencer-Smith on one of the sledges in his sleeping bag. He was quite helpless, but his courage never failed him. Steady advances were made on the next days, but although Joyce, Wild, Richards and Hayward were feeling fit Mackintosh was lame and weak, and Spencer-Smith's condition was alarming. Helped, however, by strong southerly winds, the daily distances covered were very good, and by February 12th they reached the depot at 80° S. on their return journey. Spencer-Smith seemed a little better, and all hands were cheered by the rapid advance.

February 14th, 15th and 16th were bad days owing to soft surface, and on the 18th, when the party were within twelve miles of the Bluff depot, a furious blizzard made traveling impossible. This blizzard raged for five days. Rations were reduced on the second day, and on the third day the party went on half-rations.

"Still blizzarding," Joyce wrote on the 20th. "Things are serious, what with our patient and provisions running short. . . . The most serious of calamities is that our oil is running out. We have plenty of tea, but no fuel to cook it with." The men in Mackintosh's tent were in no better plight and Mackintosh himself was in a bad way.

On the 21st Joyce wrote: "I don't know what we shall do if this does not ease. It has been blowing continuously without a lull. The food for today was one cup of pemmican among three of us, one biscuit each, and two cups of tea among the three." Twenty-four hours later he continued:

> Same old thing, no ceasing of this blizzard. Hardly any food left except tea and sugar. Richards, Hayward and I, after a long talk, decided to start tomorrow in any case, or else we shall be sharing the fate of Captain Scott and his party. The other tent seems to be very quiet, but now and again we hear a burst of song from Wild, so they are in the land of the living. We gave the dogs the last of their food tonight, so we shall have to push, as a great deal depends on them.

When, on February 23rd, they started to dig out their sledge, it took them two hours, for they found themselves terribly weak after lying up with practically no food. Further quotations from Joyce's diary tell their own story:

> Got under way about 2:20. . . . About 3:20 the Skipper, who had tied himself to the rear of the sledge, found it impossible to proceed. So, after a consultation with Wild and party, decided to pitch their tent, leaving Wild to look after the Skipper and Spencer-Smith, and make the best of our way to the depot, which is anything up to twelve miles away. So we made them comfortable and went on.
>
> I told Wild I should leave as much as possible and get back 26th or 27th, weather permitting, but just as we left them it came

on to snow pretty hard, sun going in, and even with the four dogs we could only make half to three-quarters of a mile an hour. Camped in a howling blizzard. I found my left foot badly frostbitten. Now after this march we came into our banquet— one cup of tea and half a biscuit. Situation does not look very cheerful. This is really the worst surface I have ever come across in all my journeys here.

Mackintosh had stayed on his feet as long as was humanly possible. He had been suffering for several weeks from what he cheerfully called "a sprained leg" owing to scurvy, but the responsibility for the work to be done was primarily his, and he would not give in. Spencer-Smith was sinking. Wild was in fairly good condition. Joyce, Richards and Hayward, who had undertaken the relief journey, were all showing symptoms of scurvy; their legs were weak, and their gums swollen. The decision that the invalids with Wild should stay in camp was fully justified by the circumstances. Joyce and his men had difficulty in reaching the depot with a nearly empty sledge. Any attempt to make their journey with two helpless men might have involved the loss of the whole party.

"*February* 24*th*, *Thursday*. Up at 4:30; had one cup of tea, half biscuit; under way after 7. Weather, snowing and blowing like yesterday. During forenoon had to stop every quarter of an hour on account of our breath. I wonder if this weather will ever clear up. Camped in an exhausted condition about 12:10. Lunch, half cup of weak tea and quarter biscuit, which took over half an hour to make. . . . This is the second day the dogs have been without food, and if we cannot soon pick up depot and save the dogs it will be almost impossible to drag our two invalids back the 100 miles we have to go."

Bad weather prevented the party from advancing again that day, but, in spite of everything, the men remained very cheerful.

"*February* 25*th*, *Friday*. Under way at 7; carried on, halting every ten minutes or quarter of an hour. Weather, snowing and blowing same as yesterday. We are in a very weak state, but we cannot give in. We often talk about poor Captain Scott and the blizzard that finished him and party. If we had stayed in our tent another day I don't think we should have got under way at all, and we should have shared the same fate. But if the worst comes we have made up our minds to carry on and die in harness. . . . We camped for our grand lunch at noon. After five hours' struggling I think we did about five miles. Decided to get under way as soon as there is any clearance. Snowing and blowing, force about fifty to sixty miles an hour."

"*February* 26th, *Saturday*. We got under way as soon as possible, about 2:10 AM. About 2:35 Richards sighted depot. I suppose we camped no more than three-quarters of a mile from it. The dogs sighted it, which seemed to electrify them. They had new life and started to run, but we were so weak that we could not go more than 200 yards at a spell. I think another day would have seen us off. Arrived at depot at 3:25; I don't suppose a weaker party has ever arrived at any depot, either north or south. After a hard struggle got our tent up and made camp. Then gave the dogs a good feed of pemmican. If ever dogs saved the lives of anyone they have saved ours. Let us hope they will continue in good health so that we can get out to our comrades."

The party found that none of them had any appetite although in the land of plenty, and this Joyce attributed to the reaction, and also that they found no news of the ship, which they had expected to be left there. Consequently they all thought the ship had been lost. Terrible weather followed and Joyce wrote on February 27th:

Wind continued with fury the whole night. Expecting every minute to have the tent blown off us. We are still very weak but think we can do the twelve miles to our comrades in one long march. If only it would clear up for just one day we would not mind. We have not had a traveling day for eleven days, and the amount of snow that has fallen is astonishing. *Later.* Had a meal 10:30 and decided to get under way in spite of wind and snow. Under way 12 o'clock. We have three weeks' food on sledge, about 160 lb., and one week's dog food, 50 lb. Weight, all told, about 600 lb., and also taking an extra sledge to bring back Captain Mackintosh.

Great difficulties were ahead of them. Hayward was suffering from his knees, the dogs had lost all heart in pulling. The surface was so bad that they could hardly move the sledge at times, and their pace was not more than one-half to three-quarters of a mile per hour. But they struggled on splendidly in spite of blizzards and surface, and on February 29th Joyce wrote:

"Up at 5 o'clock; still very thick. It cleared a little about 8 o'clock, and, after looking round, sighted camp to the south, so got under way as soon as possible. Got up to the camp about 12.45, when Wild came out to meet us. He told us that they had no food left. The Skipper then came out of the tent, very weak and as much as he could do to walk. He said, 'I want to thank you for saving our lives.'"

Joyce meant to start back at the earliest moment, and after lunch Mackintosh went ahead to get some exercise. Presently the party were ready to get away, and when they lifted Spencer-Smith they found that he was in a great hole which he had melted through. Soon they picked up Mackintosh, who had fallen down, being too weak to walk. They put him on the sledge they had brought out, and camped about 8 o'clock. "I think we did about three miles—rather good with two men on the sledges and Hayward in a very bad way. . . . The dogs seem to have new life since we turned north. We have now to look to southerly winds for help. Hope to try and reach depot tomorrow, even if we have to march overtime."

On March 1st and 2nd good progress on the return journey was made. "Gives one a bit of heart to carry on like this; only hope we can do this all the way." But the next day brought a raging blizzard, and they found to their disgust that it was impossible to carry on.

"*March 4th, Saturday.* Up 5:20. Still blizzarding, but have decided to get under way as Hayward is getting worse, and one doesn't know who is the next. No mistake it is scurvy, and the only possible cure is fresh food. Smith is still cheerful; he has hardly moved for weeks and he has to have everything done for him. Got under way 9:35. It took some two hours to dig out dogs and sledges, as they were completely buried. It is the same every morning now. . . . In the afternoon wind eased a bit and drift went down. Found it very hard pulling with the third man on the sledge, as Hayward has been on all the afternoon."

On March 5th and 6th a fair wind helped the party on their long way, but after lunch on the 6th the wind was not so helpful. "It seems to me," Joyce wrote, "that we shall have to depot someone if the wind eases at all."

"*March 7ᵗʰ, Tuesday*. There is double as much work to do now with our invalids. It is very hard going. Hayward and Skipper going on ahead with sticks, very slow pace. If one could only get some fresh food. After a consultation the Skipper decided to stay behind in a tent with three weeks' provisions, while we pushed on with Smith and Hayward. It seems hard, only about thirty miles away, and yet cannot get any help. Our gear is absolutely rotten; no sleep last night, shivering all night in wet bags."

On the following day they wished the Skipper "Goodbye," and took Smith and Hayward on. Fair progress was made, but a very bad night followed.

"*March 9ᵗʰ, Thursday*. At 4 AM Spencer-Smith called out that he was feeling queer. Wild spoke to him. Then at 5:45 Richards suddenly said, 'I think he has gone.' Poor Smith, for forty days in pain he had been dragged on the sledge, but never grumbled or complained. Sometimes when we lifted him on the sledge he would nearly faint, but he never complained. Wild looked after him from the start. We buried him in his bag at 9 o'clock at the following position: Ereb. 184°—Obs. Hill 149°. We made a cross of bamboos and built a mound and cairn, with particulars."

Then they got under way again and found the going very hard. "We carried on with Hayward on sledge and camped in the dark about 8 o'clock. Turned in at 10, weary, worn and sad. Hoping to reach depot tomorrow."

Eventually the party arrived at Hut Point about 3 PM on Saturday, March 11ᵗʰ, after a terribly strenuous and anxious time.

It seems strange after our adventures to arrive back at the old hut. This place has been standing since we built it in 1901, and has been the starting point of a few expeditions since. . . . Hut half full of snow through a window being left open and drift getting in; but we soon got it shipshape and Hayward in. . . . As there is no news here of the ship, and we cannot see her, we surmise she has gone down with all hands. I don't know how the Skipper will take it.

The following night all hands suffered from overeating, and all of them were also suffering from more serious trouble. Hayward could hardly move; Joyce's ankles and knees were badly swollen, and his gums prominent; Wild was very black around joints and gums very black. "After digging hut out I prepared food which I think will keep the scurvy down. The dogs have lost their lassitude and are quite frisky." Seals were plentiful and some were killed and cooked in preparation for their journey to bring in Mackintosh. They started again on March 14th, and soon after lunch on March 16th they sighted the Skipper's camp, and through glasses saw him, to everyone's joy, outside the tent. "Picked him up at 4:15 PM. Broke the news of Smith's death and no ship. He seems in a bad way. I hope to get him in in three days, and I think fresh food will improve him."

A good distance was made on the next day, and the Skipper felt much better after good food. They arrived at Hut Point at 7 PM on the following day.

Found Hayward still about the same. Now we have arrived and got the party in it remains to themselves to get better. Plenty of exercise and fresh food ought to do miracles. We have been out 160 days, and done a distance of 1,561 miles; a good record. Before turning in the Skipper shook us by the hand with great emotion, thanking us for saving his life. I think the irony of late was poor Smith going under so short a time before we got in.

This account would be incomplete without mentioning the unselfish service rendered by Wild to his two ill tent-mates. From the time he stayed behind at the long blizzard till the death of Spencer-Smith he had two helpless men to attend to, and, despite his own condition, he was ever ready, night or day, to minister to their wants. This, in a temperature of –30° Fahr., at times, was no light task.

"Without the aid of four faithful friends, Oscar, Con, Gunner and Towser, the party could never have arrived back," Richards wrote.

"These dogs from November 5th accompanied the sledging parties, and, although the pace was often very slow, they adapted themselves to it. Their endurance was fine. For three whole days at one time they had not a scrap of food, and this after a period of short rations. Those who returned with them will ever remember the remarkable service they rendered."

The five men who were now at Hut Point quickly found that some of the winter months must be spent there. They had no news of the ship, and were justified in assuming that she had not returned to the Sound, since if she had done so some message would have awaited them at Hut Point, if not farther south. The party must wait until the new ice became firm as far as Cape Evans. With plenty of fresh food and dried vegetables available the patients improved rapidly.

A tally of the stores at the hut showed that on a reasonable allowance the supply would last till the middle of June. Plenty of seals and a few penguins were killed, but the sole means of cooking food was an improvised stove of brick which emitted dense smoke, and covered the men and all their gear with clinging and penetrating soot. Cleanliness was impossible, and this increased the men's desire to get across to Cape Evans. During April the sea froze in calm weather, but winds took the ice out again. A spell of calm weather came during the first week of May and the sea-ice formed rapidly. The men made several short trips over it to the north.

The disaster that followed is described thus by Richards. "And now a most regrettable incident occurred," he wrote. "On the morning of May 8th, before breakfast, Captain Mackintosh asked Joyce what he thought of his going to Cape Evans with Hayward. Captain Mackintosh thought the ice quite safe. He was strongly urged at the time not to take the risk, as it was pointed out that the ice, although firm, was very young, and that a blizzard was almost sure to take part of it out to sea."

Mackintosh naturally would be anxious to know if the men at Cape Evans were well and if they had any news of the ship. At 1 PM, with the weather apparently changing for the worse, he and Hayward left, after promising to turn back if the weather grew worse. At 3 PM a moderate blizzard was raging which later on increased in fury, and the hut party had many misgivings for the safety of the absent men.

On May 10th, the first day possible, the three men left behind walked over new ice to the north to try and find some trace of the others. The footmarks were seen clearly enough raised up on the ice, and the track was followed for about two miles towards Cape Evans. Here they ended abruptly, and in the dim light a wide stretch of water, very lightly covered with ice, was seen as far as the eye could reach. It was at once evident that part of the ice over which they had traveled had gone out to sea. That Mackintosh and Hayward were actually lost was learned only on July 15th, when the party from Hut Point reached Cape Evans.

The entry in Joyce's diary shows that he had very strong forebodings of disaster when Mackintosh and Hayward left. Indeed he warned them not to go. The weather during June was persistently bad, and it was not until July 15th that the party could start for Cape Evans. They expected to have the help of a full moon, but by a strange chance they had chosen the period of an eclipse. They, however, reached Cape Evans without difficulty, and found Stevens, Cope, Gaze and Jack at the Cape Evans hut. Nothing had been seen of Captain Mackintosh and Hayward. The conclusion that they had perished was reluctantly accepted.

The men now settled down to wait for relief. When opportunity offered, Joyce led search parties to look for the bodies or any trace of the missing men, but in spite of determined efforts these expeditions were entirely unsuccessful. In September Richards was forced to lay up with a strained heart, and in the same month Joyce, Gaze and Wild went out to Spencer-Smith's grave with a wooden cross, which they erected firmly.

Relief arrived on January 10th, 1917, but it is necessary now to turn back to the events of May 1915, when the *Aurora* was driven from her moorings.

CHAPTER TWENTY

THE AURORA'S DRIFT

AFTER MACKINTOSH LEFT THE *AURORA* ON JANUARY 25th, 1915, Stenhouse had considerable difficulties with the ship which were successfully overcome. The break-away from the shore came suddenly and unexpectedly on the evening of May 6th. On that day Stenhouse wrote:

> 4 PM. Wind freshening with blizzardly appearance of sky. 8 PM. Heavy strain on after-moorings. 9:45 PM. The ice parted from the shore; all moorings parted. . . . In the thick haze I saw the ice astern breaking up and the shore receding. I called all hands and clapped relieving tackles on to the cables on the fore part of the windlass. The bos'n had rushed along with his hurricane lamp, and shouted, "She's away wi' it!" I ordered steam on main engines, and the engine-room staff, with Hooke and Ninnis, turned to. Grady, fireman, was laid up with a broken rib. As the ship, in the solid floe, set to the northwest, the cables rattled and tore at the hawse-pipes; luckily the anchors, lying as they were on a strip-sloping bottom, came away easily, without damage to windlass or hawse-pipes.
>
> Slowly as we disappeared into the Sound the light in the hut died away. At 11:30 PM the ice around us started to break up, the floes playing tattoo on the ship's sides. We were out in the Sound and catching the full force of the wind. . . . As the pack

from the southward came up and closed in on the ship the swell lessened and the banging of floes alongside eased a little.

"*May 7th*. Moderate gale with thick drift. The ice around is packing up and forming ridges 2 feet high. When steam is raised I have hopes of getting back to the fast ice near the Glacier Tongue." At first the engineers had great difficulties with the sea connections, but these were overcome, and presently fires were lit in the furnaces, and water began to blow in the boiler. Throughout May 7th the *Aurora* drifted helplessly and on May 8th she was moving northwards with the ice. The wind freshened to a moderate southerly gale, with thick drift, in the night, and this gale continued during the following day.

"Cape Bird is the only land visible, bearing northeast true about eight miles distant," Stenhouse wrote on the afternoon of the 9th,

. . . so this is the end of our attempt to winter in McMurdo Sound. Hard luck after four months' buffeting, for the last seven weeks of which we nursed our moorings. Our present situation calls for increasing vigilance. It is five weeks to the middle of winter. There is no sun, the light is little and uncertain, and we may expect many blizzards. We have no immediate water supply, as only a small quantity of fresh ice was aboard when we broke drift.

The *Aurora* is fast in the pack and drifting God knows where. We have good spirits and will get through. But what of the poor beggars at Cape Evans, and the Southern Party. It is a dismal prospect for them. There are enough provisions, but we have the remaining Burberry's, clothing, etc., for next year's sledging still aboard. I see little prospect of getting back to Cape Evans, or anywhere in the Sound. We are short of coal and held firmly in the ice. I hope she drifts quickly to the northeast, then we can try to push through the pack and make for New Zealand, coal and return to the Barrier east of Cape Crozier. This could be done, I think, in the early spring, September. We must get back to aid the depot-laying next season.

A violent blizzard raged on May 10th and 11th. "I never remember such wind-force; it was difficult to get along the deck." Stenhouse had had the wireless aerial rigged and tried to communicate with Macquarie Island Wireless Station (1,340 miles away) or the Bluff (New Zealand, 1,860 miles) but had no luck.

The anchors were hove in by dint of much effort on the 13th and 14th. Both anchors were broken, so the ship had only one small kedge-anchor left aboard. The record of the early months of the *Aurora's* long drift in the Ross Sea is not eventful. The ship was quite helpless in the grip of the ice, and after the engine-room bilges had been thawed and pumped out the boilers were blown down. The story of the *Aurora's* drift can be told very briefly by extracts from Stenhouse's log.

"*May* 21st. Unable to get bearing, but imagine there is little or no alteration in ship's position, as ship's head is same, and Western Mountains appear the same. Hope all is well at Cape Evans and that the other parties have returned safely. Wish we could relieve their anxiety."

"*May* 24th. Blizzard from south-southeast. Quite a lot of havoc has been caused during this blow, and the ship has made much northing. At 2 PM felt heavy shock and the ship heeled to port about 70°. Ship badly jammed in."

"*May* 25th. In middle watch felt pressure occasionally. As far as can be seen there are heavy blocks of ice screwed up on end, and the scene is like a graveyard. So near to Cape Evans, and yet we might as well be anywhere as here. Have made our sledging-ration scales, and crew are busy making harness and getting sledging equipment ready for emergencies."

"*May* 26th. If the ship is nipped in the ice, the ship's company (eighteen hands) will take to four sledges with one month's rations and make for nearest land. If the ice sets north and takes the ship clear of land we will proceed to New Zealand and return as soon as possible."

"*June* 8th. Made our latitude 75° 59′ S. by altitude of Sirius. This is a very monotonous life, but all hands appear to be happy and contented. Find that we are not too well off for meals and will have to cut rations a little."

"*June* 22nd. Today the sun has reached the limit of his northern declination, and now he will start to come south. Observed this day as a holiday."

"*July* 1*st*. The 1st of July! Thank God. Through all my waking hours one long thought of the people at Cape Evans, but one must appear to be happy and take interest in the small happenings of shipboard."

"*July* 6*th*. This morning a lane was distinctly visible and appeared to be 200 or 300 yards wide and two miles long. At 6 PM loud pressure-noises were heard from the direction of the open lane and continued through the night. The incessant grinding and grating of the ice to the southward, with seething noises, as of water rushing under the ship's bottom, and ominous sounds, kept me on the *qui vive* all night, and the prospect of a break-up of the ice would have racked my nerves had I not had them numbed by previous experiences."

"*July* 9*th*. Ship's position is twenty-eight miles north-northeast of Franklin Island. On the port bow and ahead of the ship there are some enormous pressure-ridges. Pressure heard from the southward all day."

"*July* 13*th*. Very heavy pressure was heard quite close to the ship; the ice could be seen bending upwards, and occasional jars were felt on board. I am inclined to think that we shall now experience the full force of pressure from the south. We have prepared for the worst and can only hope for the best—a release from the ice with a seaworthy vessel under us."

Heavy pressure was frequent during the following days, and on July 21st the rudder was bent over to starboard and smashed, the solid oak and iron going like matchwood. On July 22nd Stenhouse wrote:

Ship in bad position in newly frozen lane, with bow and stern jammed against heavy floes; heavy strain with much creaking and groaning. 8 AM. Called all hands to stations for sledges, and made final preparations for abandoning ship. Allotted special duties to several hands to facilitate quickness in getting clear should ship be crushed. Am afraid the ship's back will be broken if the pressure continues, but cannot relieve her . . . 12 PM. Ship is in safer position, lanes opening in every direction.

"*July* 23*rd*. The ship's stern is now in a more or less soft bed, formed of recently frozen ice of about 1 foot in thickness. I thank God that we have been spared through this fearful nightmare. I shall never forget the concertina motions of the ship during yesterday's and Wednesday's fore and aft nips."

July 24th was a comparatively quiet day, but very heavy pressure about the ship occurred on the 25th. During the early hours a large field on the port quarter came charging up, and on meeting the *Aurora's* floe tossed up a ridge from 10 to 15 feet high. The blocks of ice as they broke off crumbled and piled over each other to the accompaniment of a thunderous roar. Pressure continued all the day, the floes opening and closing alternately, and the ship creaking and groaning during the nips between the floes.

"*August 4th*. For nine days we have had southerly winds, and the last four we have experienced howling blizzards. I am sick of the sound of the infernal wind."

"*August 6th*. After four days of thick weather we find ourselves in sight of Cape Adare in a position about forty-five miles east of Possession Isles. We felt excited this morning in anticipation of seeing the sun. It was a glorious, joyful sight. We drank to something, and with very light hearts gave cheers for the sun."

"*August 9th*. Donolly got to work on the rudder again. It is a long job cutting through the iron sheathing-plates of the rudder, and not too safe at present, as the ice is treacherous."

"*August 10th*. The ship's position is lat. 70° 40′ S. The distance drifted from August 2nd to 6th was 100 miles, and from the 6th to 10th eighty-eight miles."

"*August 12th*. By observation and bearings of land we are forty-five miles northeast of Cape Adare. Donolly and Grady are having quite a job with the iron platings on the rudder, but should finish the cutting tomorrow. A jury-rudder is nearly completed. The carpenter has made a good job of the rudder, although he has had to construct it on the quarter-deck in low temperatures and exposed to biting blasts."

"*August 24th*. We lifted the rudder out of the ice and placed it clear of the stern, athwart the fore-and-aft line of the ship. We had quite a job with it (weight, 4 ½ tons). I am glad to see the rudder upon the ice and clear of the propeller."

"*August 25th*. Hooke has just been in with the good news that he has heard Macquarie and the Bluff (New Zealand) sending their weather reports and exchanging signals. Can this mean they have heard the signals which Hooke has been sending, and are trying to get us now?" (It was learned afterwards that no wireless messages from the *Aurora* had been received by any station.)

"*August* 31st. Very loud pressure-noises to the southeast. I went aloft after breakfast and had the pleasure of seeing many open lanes in all directions. The lanes of yesterday are frozen over, showing what little chance there is of a general and continued break-up of the ice until the temperature rises. We cannot get out of this too quickly."

"*September* 5th. The mizen wireless mast came down in a raging blizzard today. Luckily, as it is dangerous to life to be on deck in this weather, no one was about when the mast carried away."

"*September* 8th. This is dull, miserable weather. Sometimes it blows in this neighborhood without snow and sometimes with—this seems to be the only difference."

"*September* 9th. This is the first day for a long time we have registered a minimum temperature above zero for the twenty-four hours. With the increase of daylight it makes one feel that summer is really approaching."

"*September* 17th. This is the anniversary of our departure from London. Much has happened since Friday, September 18th, 1914, and I can recall the scene as we passed down the Thames with submarines and cruisers, in commission and bent on business, crossing our course. I can also remember the regret at leaving it all, and the consequent 'fed-upness.'"

"*September* 22nd. Since breaking away from Cape Evans we have drifted roughly 705 miles around islands and past formidable obstacles, a wonderful drift. It is good to think that it has not been in vain, and that the knowledge of the set and drift of the pack will be a valuable addition to the sum of human knowledge."

During the month of October the *Aurora* drifted uneventfully, but anxious eyes were strained in vain for indications that the day of the ship's release was near at hand. The floe, however, into which the ship was frozen, remained firm until the early days of November. The temperatures were higher now under the influence of the sun, and the ice was softer. There was a pronounced thaw on the 22nd. Stenhouse thought that a stiff blizzard would break up the pack. His anxiety was increasing with the advance of the season, and his log is a record of deep yearning to be free and active again. But the grip of the pack was inexorable. The jury-rudder was ready to be shipped when the ship was released, but meanwhile it was not being exposed to the attack of the ice. "No appreciable change in our surroundings," was the note for December 17th, and Christmas Day, with its special dinner and mild festivities, came and passed with the ice still firm.

At the end of the first week in January the ship was in lat. 65° 45′ S. The pack was well broken a mile from the ship, and the ice was rolling fast. The middle of January passed, however, and the *Aurora* lay still in the ice. The period of continuous day was drawing to a close, and at midnight there was an appreciable twilight. Stenhouse ordered a thorough overhaul of the stores and general preparations for a move. The supply of flour and butter was ample, but other stores were running low, and no chance was lost of capturing seals and penguins.

The break-up of the floe in which the *Aurora* was held came on February 12th. Strong winds put the ice in motion and brought a perceptible swell. The ship was making some water, a foretaste of trouble to come, and all hands spent the day at the pumps. Work had just finished for the night when the ice broke astern and quickly split in all directions. The ship was floating now amid fragments of floe, and bumping considerably in the swell. A fresh southerly wind blew during the night, and the ship started to forge ahead gradually without sail. On the morning of the 13th Stenhouse set the foresail and fore-topmast staysail, and the *Aurora* moved northward slowly, being brought up occasionally by large floes.

Navigation under such conditions, without steam or rudder, was very difficult, but Stenhouse wished if possible to save his small remaining stock of coal until he cleared the pack, so that a quick run might be made to McMurdo Sound. The jury-rudder could not be rigged in the pack. The ship was making about 3½ feet of water in the twenty-four hours, a quantity easily checked by the pumps.

During the 14th the *Aurora* worked very slowly northward through heavy pack, but the ship was held up all day on the 15th, heavy floes barring progress in all directions. This state of affairs continued on the 16th, and, with a heavy swell rolling under the ice, the ship had a rough time. "I am afraid," Stenhouse wrote, "our chances of getting south are very small now."

The pack remained close, and on the 21st a heavy swell made the situation dangerous. On the night of the 25th the pack loosened, and a heavy northwest swell caused the ship to bump heavily. This state of affairs recurred at intervals in succeeding days. On the 29th Stenhouse wrote: "The battering and ramming of the floes increased in the early hours until it seemed as if some sharp floe or jagged underfoot must go through the ship's hull. . . . I am anxious about the propeller. This pack is a dangerous place for a ship now; it seems miraculous that the old Barky still floats."

The ice opened out a little on March 1st. Winter was approaching and it was imperative to get the ship out of her dangerous situation, and therefore Stenhouse ordered steam to be raised. But progress was very slow owing to heavy floes and deep underfoots, which necessitated frequent stoppages of the engines. Before noon on the 3rd the ship came to a full stop among heavy floes, and Stenhouse had the fires partially drawn (to save coal) and banked.

No advance was made on March 4th and 5th. A moderate gale closed the ice and set it in motion, and the *Aurora*, with banked fires, rolled and bumped heavily. Seventeen bergs were in sight, and one of them was working southwards into the pack and threatening to approach the ship. "All theories about the swell being non-existent in the pack are false," the anxious master wrote. "Here we are with a suggestion only of open water-sky, and the ship rolling her scuppers under and sitting down bodily on the floes." The ice opened when the wind moderated, and on the 6th the *Aurora* moved northward again.

The next three days were full of anxiety. The ship was again held by the ice and severely buffeted, while two bergs approached from the north. On the 10th the nearest berg was within three cables of the ship, but the pack opened and the ship got clear of the danger zone. During the afternoon the pack continued to open, and the *Aurora* passed through wide stretches of small loose floes and brash. She was once more bumped severely during the night.

Early next morning Stenhouse lowered a jury-rudder and moved north to northwest through heavy pack. In the late afternoon of the

13th the ship cleared the main pack but bergs and growlers were a constant menace during the hours of darkness. Anxious work remained to be done, since bergs and scattered ice extended in all directions, but at 2 PM on March 14th the *Aurora* cleared the last belt of pack in lat. 62° 27.5′ S., long. 157° 32′ E. "We 'spliced the main brace,'" says Stenhouse, "and blew three blasts of farewell to the pack with the whistle."

The *Aurora* was not at the end of her troubles, but the voyage to New Zealand need not be described in detail. Any attempt to reach McMurdo Sound was now out of the question. Stenhouse had a battered, rudderless ship, with only a few tons of coal left, and he struggled northward in heavy weather against persistent adverse winds and head seas. The jury-rudder required constant nursing, and the coal shortage made it impossible to get the best service from the engines. At times the ship could make no progress, and fell about helplessly in a confused swell or lay hove to amid mountainous seas. She was short-handed, and one or two of the men created additional difficulties. But Stenhouse displayed throughout fine seamanship and dogged perseverance.

He accomplished successfully one of the most difficult voyages on record, in an ocean area notoriously stormy and treacherous. On March 23rd he established wireless communication with Bluff Station, New Zealand, and the next day was in touch with Wellington and Hobart. The naval officer in New Zealand waters offered assistance, and eventually it was arranged that the Otago Harbor Board's tug *Plucky* should meet the *Aurora* outside Port Chalmers.

There were still bad days to be endured. The jury-rudder partially carried away and had to be unshipped in a heavy sea. Stenhouse carried on, and on April 2nd the *Aurora* picked up the tug and was taken in tow. She reached Port Chalmers on the following morning, and was welcomed with the warm hospitality which New Zealand has always shown towards Antarctic explorers.

CHAPTER TWENTY-ONE

THE LAST RELIEF

WHEN I REACHED NEW ZEALAND AT THE BEGINNING OF DECEMBER 1916, I found that arrangements for relief were complete. The New Zealand government had taken the task in hand before I had got into touch with the outside world. The British and Australian governments were giving financial assistance. The *Aurora* had been repaired and refitted at Port Chalmers during the year, and had been provisioned and coaled for the voyage to McMurdo Sound.

My old friend, Captain John K. Davis, a member of my first Antarctic expedition in 1907–1909, and who subsequently commanded Dr. Mawson's ship in the Australian Antarctic expedition, had been placed in command of the *Aurora* by the governments, and he had engaged officers, engineers and crew. Captain Davis came to see me on my arrival at Wellington, and I heard his account of the position. Stenhouse also was in Wellington, and I may say again here that his account of his voyage and drift in the *Aurora* filled me with admiration for his pluck, seamanship and resourcefulness.

After discussing the situation with the Minister for Marine, Dr. McNab, who took a deep personal interest in the expedition, I agreed that all arrangements for the relief expedition should stand. Time was precious and there were difficulties about changing plans or control at the last moment. After Captain Davis had been at work for some months the government agreed to hand the *Aurora* over to me free of liability on her return to New Zealand.

It was decided, therefore, that Captain Davis should take the ship down to McMurdo Sound, and that I should go with him to take charge of any shore operations which might be necessary. I "signed on" at a salary of 1ˢ. a month, and we sailed from Port Chalmers on December 20ᵗʰ, 1916.

After a fairly quick passage Captain Davis brought the *Aurora* alongside the ice edge off Cape Royds on the morning of January 10ᵗʰ, and I went ashore with a party to look for some record in the hut erected there by my expedition in 1907. I found a letter stating that the Ross Sea party were at Cape Evans, and was on my way back to the ship when six men, with dogs and sledge, were sighted coming from the direction of Cape Evans. At 1 PM this party arrived on board, and they told us of the deaths of Mackintosh, Spencer-Smith and Hayward, and of their own anxious wait for relief. The seven survivors, namely, A. Stevens, E. Joyce, H. E. Wild, J. L. Cope, R. W. Richards, A. K. Jack, I. O. Gaze, were all well, though showing traces of the ordeal through which they had passed.

All that remained to be done was to make a final search for the bodies of Mackintosh and Hayward. There was no possibility whatever of either man being alive. Joyce had already searched south of Glacier Tongue. I thought that further search should be made in the area north of Glacier Tongue, and the old depot off Butter Point, and I made a report to Captain Davis to this effect.

On January 12ᵗʰ the ship reached a point five and a half miles east of Butter Point. I took a party across rubbly and water-logged ice to within thirty yards of the piedmont ice, but owing to high cliffs and loose slushy ice we could not make a landing. There was no sign of the depot or of any person having visited the vicinity. We returned to the ship and proceeded across the Sound to Cape Bernacchi.

The next day I took a party ashore to search the area north of Glacier Tongue, including Razorback Island, but these efforts were in vain. On the 15ᵗʰ a southeast blizzard prevented us from sledging, and we spent the day in putting the hut at Cape Evans in order. On the 16ᵗʰ Joyce and I went to Glacier Tongue, but we could see from the top that there was not the slightest chance of finding any remains owing to the enormous snowdrifts wherever the cliffs were accessible. The base of the steep cliffs had drifts 10 to 15 feet high. I considered that all places likely to hold the bodies of Mackintosh and Hayward had now been searched, and, after reaching the hut that night at 9:40, we left almost immediately for the ship. During our absence from the hut Wild and Jack had erected a cross to the memory of the three men who had lost their lives in the service of the expedition.

Captain Davis took the ship northward on January 17th, and on February 9th the *Aurora* was berthed at Wellington. We were welcomed like returned brothers by the New Zealand people.

CHAPTER TWENTY-TWO

THE FINAL PHASE

THE FOREGOING CHAPTERS OF THIS BOOK REPRESENT THE GENERAL narrative of our expedition. That we failed to accomplish the object we set out for was due, I consider, not to any neglect or lack of organization, but to the overwhelming natural obstacles, especially the unprecedented severe summer conditions on the Weddell Sea side. But, though the expedition failed in one respect, it was, I think, successful in many others. A large amount of important scientific work was carried out; the meteorological observations in particular have an economic bearing. The hydrographical work in the Weddell Sea has done much to clear up the mystery of this, the least known of all the seas.

To the credit side of the expedition one can safely say that the comradeship and resource of the members of the expedition was worthy of the highest traditions of Polar service; and it was a privilege to me to have under my command men who, through dark days and the stress and strain of continuous danger, kept up their spirits and carried out their work regardless of themselves and heedless of the limelight.

The same energy and endurance which they showed in the Antarctic they brought to the Greater War in the Old World. And having followed our fortunes in the South it may interest you to know that practically every member of the expedition was employed in one or other branches of the active fighting forces during the war. Of the fifty-three men who returned out of the fifty-six who left for the South, three have since been killed and five wounded. McCarthy, the best

and most efficient of the sailors, always cheerful under the most trying circumstances, and who for these reasons I chose to accompany
me on the boat journey to South Georgia, was killed at his gun in
the Channel. Cheetham, the veteran of the Antarctic, who had been
more often south of the Antarctic Circle than any man, was drowned
when the vessel in which he was serving was torpedoed a few weeks
before the Armistice.

Ernest Wild, Frank Wild's brother, was killed while minesweeping
in the Mediterranean. Manger, the carpenter on the *Aurora*, was badly
wounded while serving with the New Zealand Infantry. The two surgeons, Macklin and McIlroy, served in France and Italy, McIlroy being
badly wounded at Ypres. Frank Wild, in view of his unique experience
of ice and ice conditions, was at once sent to the North Russian front,
where his zeal and ability won him the highest praise. Macklin served
first with the Yorks and later transferred as medical officer to the
Tanks, where he did much good work. Going to the Italian front with
his battalion, he won the Military Cross for bravery in tending wounded
under fire.

James joined the Royal Engineers, Sound-Ranging Section, and
after much frontline work was given charge of a Sound-Ranging School
to teach other officers this latest and most scientific addition to the art
of war. Wordie went to France with the Royal Field Artillery and was
badly wounded at Armentières.

Hussey was in France for eighteen months with the Royal Garrison
Artillery, serving in every big battle from Dixmude to Saint-Quentin.
Worsley, known to his intimates as Depth-Charge Bill, owing to his success with that particular method of destroying German submarines,
has the D. S. O. and three submarines to his credit.

Stenhouse was with Worsley as his second in command when one
of the German submarines was rammed and sunk, and received the
D. S. C. for his share in the fight. He was afterwards given command
of a Mystery Ship, and fought several actions with enemy submarines.

Clark served on a minesweeper. Greenstreet was employed with the
barges on the Tigris. Rickenson was commissioned as Engineer-
Lieutenant, R. N. Kerr returned to the Merchant Service as an engineer.

Most of the crew of the *Endurance* served on minesweepers.

Of the Ross Sea Party, Mackintosh, Hayward and Spencer-Smith died for their country as surely as those who gave up their lives in France or Flanders. Hooke, the wireless operator, became navigator of an airship.

Nearly all the crew of the *Aurora* joined the New Zealand Field Forces and saw active service in one of the many theaters of war.

Four decorations have been won, and several members of the expedition have been mentioned in dispatches.

On my return, after the rescue of the survivors of the Ross Sea Party, I offered my services to the government, and was sent on a mission to South America. When this was concluded I was commissioned as Major and went to North Russia in charge of Arctic Equipment and Transport, having with me Worsley, Stenhouse, Hussey, Macklin and Brocklehurst, who was to have come South with us, but who, as a regular officer, rejoined his unit on the outbreak of war.

Worsley was sent across to the Archangel front, where he did excellent work, and the others served with me on the Murmansk front. The mobile columns there had exactly the same clothing, equipment and sledging food as we had on the expedition. No expense was spared to get the best of everything for them, and consequently not a single case of avoidable frostbite was reported.

Taking the expedition as a unit, out of fifty-six men, three died in the Antarctic, three were killed in action and five have been wounded, so that our casualties have been fairly high.

Though some have gone, there are enough left to rally round and form a nucleus for the next expedition; when troublous times are over and scientific exploration can once more be legitimately undertaken.

INDEX

SUGGESTED READING

ALEXANDER, CAROLINE. *The Endurance: Shackleton's Legendary Antarctic Expedition*. New York: Knopf, 1998.

———. *Mrs. Chippy's Last Expedition: The Remarkable Journal of Shackleton's Polar-Bound Cat*. New York: Harper Collins, 1997.

AMUNDSEN, ROALD. *The South Pole*. New York: Cooper Square Press, 2001.

BANCROFT, ANN, AND LIV ARNESEN. *No Horizon Is So Far: Two Women and Their Extraordinary Journey across Antarctica*. New York: Penguin, 2004.

BICKEL, LENNARD. *Shackleton's Forgotten Men: The Untold Tragedy of the Endurance Epic*. New York: Thunder's Mouth Press, 2000.

———. *Mawson's Will: The Greatest Polar Survival Story Ever Written*. New York: Stein & Day, 1977.

CHERRY-GARRARD, APSLEY. *The Worst Journey in the World*. New York: Barnes & Noble, 2004.

DARLINGTON, JENNIE. *My Antarctic Honeymoon*. Garden City, NY: Doubleday, 1956.

DUNNETT, HARDING, MCGREGOR. *Shackleton's Boat: The Story of the James Caird*. Dulwich College, London: The James Caird Society, 1996.

FOX, WILLIAM. *Terra Antarctica: Looking into the Emptiest Continent*. San Antonio, TX: Trinity University Press, 2005.

HEACOX, KIM. *Shackleton: The Antarctic Challenge*. Washington, DC: National Geographic, 1995.

HUNTFORD, ROLAND. *Shackleton*. New York: Atheneum, 1986.

———. *Scott & Amundsen*. New York: Putnam, 1979.

HURLEY, FRANK. *South with Endurance: Shackleton's Antarctic Expedition of 1914–1917: The Photographs of Frank Hurley*. New York: Simon & Schuster, 2001.

————. *Argonauts of the South—Being a Narrative of Voyaging and Polar Seas and Adventures in the Antarctic with Sir Douglas Mawson and Sir Ernest Shackleton with 75 Illustrations and Maps.* New York: Putnam, 1925.

LANSING, ALFRED. *Endurance: Shackleton's Incredible Voyage.* New York: Avon, 1960.

LEGLER, GRETCHEN. *On the Ice: An Intimate Portrait of Life at McMurdo Station, Antarctica.* Minneapolis: Milkweed Editions, 2004.

MATTHIESSEN, PETER. *End of the Earth: Voyages in Antarctica.* Washington, DC: National Geographic, 2004.

MORELL, MARGOT, AND STEPHANIE CAPPARELL. *Shackleton's Way: Leadership Lessons from the Great Antarctic Explorer.* New York: Viking, 2001.

NIELSEN, JERRI. *Icebound: A Doctor's Incredible Battle for Survival at the South Pole.* New York: Hyperion, 2001.

SCOTT, ROBERT FALCON. *Scott's Last Expedition: The Journals.* New York: Carroll & Graff, 1996.

SHACKLETON, ERNEST. *The Heart of the Antarctic: Being the Story of the British Antarctic Expedition 1907–1909.* New York: Carroll & Graff, 1999.

WHEELER, SARA. *Cherry: A Life of Apsley Cherry-Garrard.* New York: Random House, 2002.

WORSLEY, FRANK. *Shackleton's Boat Journey.* New York: Norton, 1998.

————. *Endurance: An Epic of Polar Adventure.* New York: J. Cape and H. Smith, 1931.

Look for the following titles, available now from
The Barnes & Noble Library of Essential Reading.

Visit your Barnes & Noble bookstore,
or shop online at *www.bn.com/loer*

NONFICTION

Age of Reason, The	Thomas Paine	0760778957
Age of Revolution, The	Winston S. Churchill	0760768595
Alexander	Theodore Ayrault Dodge	0760773491
American Indian Stories	Zitkala-Ša	0760765502
Ancient Greek Historians, The	J. B. Bury	0760776350
Annals of Imperial Rome, The	Tacitus	0760788898
Antichrist, The	Friedrich Nietzsche	0760777705
Autobiography of Benjamin Franklin, The	Benjamin Franklin	0760768617
Autobiography of Charles Darwin, The	Charles Darwin	0760769087
Babylonian Life and History	E. A. Wallis Budge	0760765499
Beyond the Pleasure Principle	Sigmund Freud	0760774919
Birth of Britain, The	Winston S. Churchill	0760768579
Birth of Tragedy, The	Friedrich Nietzsche	0760780862
Century of Dishonor, A	Helen Hunt Jackson	0760778973
Characters and Events of Roman History	Guglielmo Ferrero	0760765928
Chemical History of a Candle, The	Michael Faraday	0760765227
City of God, The	Saint Augustine	0760779023
Civil War, The	Julius Caesar	0760768943
Common Law, The	Oliver Wendell Holmes	0760754985
Confessions	Jean-Jacques Rousseau	0760773599
Conquest of Gaul, The	Julius Caesar	0760768951

Treatise of Human Nature, A	David Hume	0760771723
Trial and Death of Socrates, The	Plato	0760762007
Twelve Years a Slave	Solomon Northup	0760783349
Up From Slavery	Booker T. Washington	0760752346
Utilitarianism	John Stuart Mill	0760771758
Vindication of the Rights of Woman, A	Mary Wollstonecraft	0760754942
Voyage of the Beagle, The	Charles Darwin	0760754969
Wealth of Nations, The	Adam Smith	0760757615
Wilderness Hunter, The	Theodore Roosevelt	0760756031
Will to Believe and Human Immortality, The	William James	0760770190
Will to Power, The	Friedrich Nietzsche	0760777772
Worst Journey in the World, The	Aspley Cherry-Garrard	0760757593

FICTION AND LITERATURE

Abbott, Edwin A.	Flatland	0760755876
Austen, Jane	Love and Freindship	0760768560
Braddon, Mary Elizabeth	Lady Audley's Secret	0760763046
Bronte, Charlotte	Professor, The	0760768854
Burroughs, Edgar Rice	Land that Time Forgot, The	0760768862
Burroughs, Edgar Rice	Martian Tales Trilogy, The	076075585X
Butler, Samuel	Way of All Flesh, The	0760765855
Castiglione, Baldesar	Book of the Courtier, The	0760768323
Cather, Willa	Alexander's Bridge	0760768870
Cather, Willa	One of Ours	0760777683
Chaucer, Geoffrey	Troilus and Criseyde	0760768919
Chesterton, G. K.	Ball and the Cross, The	0760783284
Chesterton, G. K.	Innocence and Wisdom of Father Brown, The	0760773556
Chesterton, G. K.	Man Who Was Thursday, The	0760763100
Childers, Erskine	Riddle of the Sands, The	0760765235
Cleland, John	Fanny Hill	076076591X
Conrad, Joseph	Secret Agent, The	0760783217
Cooper, James Fenimore	Pioneers, The	0760779015
Cummings, E. E.	Enormous Room, The	076077904X
Defoe, Daniel	Journal of the Plague Year, A	0760752370
Dos Passos, John	Three Soldiers	0760757542
Doyle, Arthur Conan	Complete Brigadier Gerard, The	0760768897
Doyle, Arthur Conan	Lost World, The	0760755833
Doyle, Arthur Conan	White Company and Sir Nigel, The	0760768900

Trollope, Anthony	Warden, The	0760773610
Twain, Mark	Tramp Abroad, A	0760773629
Verne, Jules	From the Earth to the Moon	0760765197
Wallace, Lew	Ben-Hur	0760763062
Walpole, Horace	Castle of Otranto, The	0760763070
Whitman, Walt	Specimen Days	0760791139
Wells, H. G.	Island of Doctor Moreau, The	0760755841
Woolf, Virginia	Jacob's Room	0760778981
Zola, Emile	Ladies' Paradise, The	0760777675

THE BARNES & NOBLE
LIBRARY OF ESSENTIAL READING

This series has been established to provide affordable access to books of literary, academic, and historic value—works of both well-known writers and those who deserve to be rediscovered. Selected and introduced by scholars and specialists with an intimate knowledge of the works, these volumes present complete, original texts in a modern, readable typeface—welcoming a new generation of readers to influential and important books of the past. With more than 300 titles already in print and more than 100 forthcoming, the Library of Essential Reading offers an unrivaled variety of thought, scholarship, and entertainment. Best of all, these handsome and durable paperbacks are priced to be exceptionally affordable. For a full list of titles, visit *www.bn.com/loer.*